A History of Hitler's Empire

Professor Thomas Childers

THE TEACHING COMPANY ®

PUBLISHED BY:

THE TEACHING COMPANY
4840 Westfields Boulevard, Suite 500
Chantilly, Virginia 20151-2299
1-800-TEACH-12
Fax—703-378-3819
www.teach12.com

ISBN 1-56585-798-4

Thomas Childers, Ph.D.

Professor of History, University of Pennsylvania

Thomas Childers was born and raised in East Tennessee. He received his bachelor's and master's degrees from the University of Tennessee and earned his Ph.D. in History from Harvard University in 1976.

Since 1976, Professor Childers has taught in the Department of History at the University of Pennsylvania. He is the recipient of numerous fellowships and awards, including a Fulbright scholarship, the Alexander von Humboldt Stiftung Research Grant, a fellowship in European Studies from the American Council of Learned Societies, and a West European Studies Research Grant from Harvard University.

During his tenure at Penn, Professor Childers has won a number of awards for his work in the classroom, including the Ira T. Abrahms Award for Distinguished Teaching and Challenging Teaching in the Arts and Sciences (1987), the Richard S. Dunn Award for Distinguished Teaching in History (1999), and the Senior Class Award for Excellence in Undergraduate Teaching (2000). The recipient of the Senior Class Award is chosen by the graduating class of the University of Pennsylvania.

In addition to teaching at Penn, Dr. Childers has held visiting professorships at Trinity Hall College, Cambridge; Smith College; and Swarthmore College and he has lectured in London, Oxford, Berlin, Munich, and at other universities in the United States and Europe.

Professor Childers is the author and editor of several books on modern German history and the Second World War. These include *The Nazi Voter* (Chapel Hill, 1983), *The Formation of the Nazi Constituency* (London, 1987), and *Reevaluating the Third Reich: New Controversies, New Interpretations* (New York, 1993). He is currently completing a trilogy on the Second World War. The first volume of that history, *Wings of Morning: The Story of the Last American Bomber Shot Down Over Germany in World War II* (Reading, Mass.: Addison-Wesley, 1995), was praised by Jonathan Yardley in *The Washington Post* as "a powerful and unselfconsciously beautiful book." The second volume, *We'll Meet*

Again (New York: Henry Holt and Company) is set for publication in the fall of 2002. The final volume, *The Best Years of Their Lives*, will follow in due course.

Table of Contents
A History of Hitler's Empire

A History of Hitler's Empire

Scope:

In these 12 lectures, we will trace the rise to power of Adolf Hitler and his Nationalist Socialist party (the NSDAP). Although we will address a wide variety of issues, these lectures pose two fundamental questions: First, how could Adolf Hitler and the Nazis come to power in such a highly educated, industrially developed country at the very heart of Western culture and civilization? This question leads to a variety of important issues: What did Germans think they were getting when they voted National Socialist? How did the Nazis present themselves to the German public? What did they seem to stand for? The second basic question deals with the Nazis in power. How were the Nazis able to establish the foundations of a totalitarian regime in such a short time and hurl Europe—and the world—into a devastating war that would consume millions of lives and change the very basis of international politics in the 20th century? Why was there apparently so little resistance? What made the regime popular at home? How were the Nazis able to seize control of the press, the radio, the courts, and the police with so little trouble?

The first six lectures of the course will be devoted to the rise of the Nazis between 1919 and 1933. We will begin our examination with a look at what might be called long-term factors that shaped German political culture in the 20th century. Specially, we will focus on the problematic nature of German national unification in 1871 and on the deep cleavages—religious divisions, lingering regional loyalties, and growing social or class tensions—that made nation building in the new Germany difficult. In this vein, we will also explore the impact of World War I on this young German state. Until the very end of the war in 1918, Germany, despite enormous casualties and sacrifices on the home front, seemed to be winning. Then, in November 1918, the roof suddenly caved in. Inexplicably to many Germans, Germany had lost the war! The new democratic government, the Weimar Republic, was forced by the victorious Allies to sign a humiliating treaty and begin its political life carrying a staggering burden. The demands of the war had widened the divisions in German society, and the new regime would have to deal with those potentially revolutionary forces as well.

The lectures then turn to more short-term factors and developments, examining, in particular, the grave economic problems confronting the Weimar governments—the chaotic hyperinflation of 1923, the harsh stabilization of 1924, and the Great Depression, with its failed businesses and skyrocketing unemployment. We will see how the NSDAP, using negative campaigning and revolutionary propaganda techniques, was able to exploit this series of devastating economic developments and the failure of the Weimar government to deal effectively with them. We will analyze the party's appeal to the electorate, examining its innovative approach to campaigning and the content of its appeals. Then we will attempt to determine what sort of person supported the party and why.

The second half of the course deals with the NSDAP in power, the Third Reich. These lectures begin by treating the Nazi seizure and consolidation of total power in 1933–1934. In particular, they focus on the step-by-step process by which resistance was broken and the major institutions of state and society were brought with surprising speed under Nazi control. We examine the system of terror and propaganda that solidified the new totalitarian state, a state that did not recognize the distinction between public and private and whose claim on the individual was total. By 1935, with power now firmly in Nazi hands, the ideological core of the National Socialist movement began to reveal itself. At this juncture, we will examine Hitler's racial ideas and the policies adopted to transform those ideas into reality. The focus here is largely on the Nazis' mounting repression of the Jewish population and the role of Heinrich Himmler's SS in shaping and enforcing the regime's anti-Semitic policies.

The lectures also address the sources of Hitler's popularity, especially his conduct of foreign policy between 1933 and 1939. We will examine Hitler's views on foreign policy and his systematic destruction of the Treaty of Versailles. We will show how and why he was able to outmaneuver the apprehensive Western European powers and how he entered into accommodation with his rival, Stalin, on the eve of World War II. The closing lectures are focused sharply on the coming of the Second World War, its course on the battlefield, and finally, the Holocaust. Hitler's war was not simply a traditional geopolitical conflict, a grab for land and resources; it was a racial war as well. Revealed most obviously in the ideological war against the Soviet Union, Hitler saw his enemy as a "Judeo-Bolshevist" conspiracy, which he was called on to eliminate. This meant not only a war of annihilation of the Soviet Union, but the destruction of the European Jewish community. We will follow Hitler's war against the Jews from *Mein Kampf* to Auschwitz and, finally, examine how, after so much death and destruction, his evil empire was destroyed.

Lecture One
The Third Reich, Hitler, and the 20th Century

Scope:

The National Socialist (or "Nazi") movement in Germany arose from the ashes of World War I and led to the cataclysm of World War II. Although a relatively short-lived political phenomenon, its impact on the course of 20th-century history cannot be overemphasized. This lecture will explain why it is important to study the National Socialist movement, and it will survey the European (especially the German) political context in which Nazism emerged during the early 1920s. Lecture One sets the stage for further investigation of the ideology, personalities, and life cycle of Nazi Germany.

Outline

I. We can point to several compelling reasons to study the National Socialist movement.

    A. Despite, or perhaps because of, the horrors of war and genocide that are associated with Nazi Germany, we must address, analyze, and cope with it.

    B. This political movement changed the world balance of power and altered millions of lives forever.

        1. Its victims include the millions of soldiers and civilians who lost their lives in military operations in World War II or the Holocaust, as well as those who had to endure the privations of post-war recovery and dislocation. Fifty-five million people perished during the war.

        2. The legacy of Nazi Germany included the Cold War between the Soviet Union and the United States. Germany and Berlin were divided between these superpowers for nearly 50 years.

    C. Germany is an integral part of our civilization. It has contributed immensely to Western culture for centuries in literature, music, science, and other fields of endeavor. Therefore, it is important to fit this period of history into the entire context of German history.

D. Finally, it is imperative to study the National Socialist movement because of concerns that a similar regime might rise somewhere else.

II. These lectures will consider the following short-term factors.

A. The kind of people who were attracted to the National Socialists were true believers who were ideologically committed. We need to look at the role of the Nazi ideology per se. Did these ideas themselves attract the German people? If so, what aspect of this program elicited such a strong ideological response?

B. In addressing Hitler's rise to power, we will propose answers to the following questions:

1. How did the National Socialists subvert the postwar "democratic" Weimar Republic (established in 1919 and ended in 1933)?

2. Who supported the NSDAP and why?

3. How did the Nazis outmaneuver and effectively break political opposition?

4. Why was there so little resistance to their emergence to power as a totalitarian regime?

C. We will also examine daily life in National Socialist Germany from the perspectives of average Germans and of the ultimate victims of the Nazis' racial policy.

III. These lectures will also consider the following longer-term factors.

A. First, we will examine the problematic nature of Germany's unification in 1871and its pattern of industrialization

1. German unification came very late; until the late 19th century, the history of the German nation was one of disunity and regionalism.

2. The new German state was not created on a wave of mass nationalism but was the result of Prussian military might.

B. The political system was beset by three important cleavages, or divisions: region (North and South), religion (Protestant and Catholic), and class (established middle and aristocratic classes and the working class).

C. Germany's industrialization came later than that of most other Western European countries but grew very quickly, creating strong and important social divisions.

Essential Reading:

Childers, Thomas, *The Nazi Voter: The Social Foundations of Fascism in Germany, 1919–1933*, introduction and chapter 1.

Supplementary Reading:

Mommsen, Hans, *The Weimar Republic*.

Questions to Consider:

1. What are some of the key factors or trends in Germany's past that might help us explain developments in 20th-century Germany? Do you think National Socialism is consistent with, or a deviation from, this historical background?

2. How does one explain the ongoing, indeed, passionate interest in the Third Reich over 50 years after it collapsed?

Lecture One—Transcript
The Third Reich, Hitler, and the 20th Century

Hello. Welcome to The Teaching Company's course on the History of Hitler's Empire. I'm delighted to be here today. My name is Tom Childers, and ten years ago, I was on the set doing exactly this same course, different venue. At the beginning of that course, we began by asking a series of questions, problems, issues to be confronted if one were going to—I wouldn't say so much "understand" as "come to terms with" or "cope with" the National Socialist experience, Hitler, the Third Reich, the Nazis. It's probably not surprising that at the outset of this course, we're going to begin by revisiting some of those very basic questions.

There's a story—I think apocryphal, possibly not—of a man who goes back to his old college to attend his daughter's graduation and during the festivities runs into his old history professor. The professor is delighted to see him; the man introduces himself and says, "My daughter was in your course this year, and she enjoyed it as much as I did 25 years ago. But I couldn't help noticing that the questions on the final exam are the same questions that you asked us 25 years ago." The professor smiled and said, "Yes, but the answers are all different."

I wouldn't say that the answers are all different as we come to this new evaluation, or reevaluation, of Hitler, National Socialism, and the Third Reich. Facts don't change, but we do, and our perspective on them changes. We learn new things, and as a result of this, it is necessary to reevaluate, once again examine what we have known and how it looks different to us at this particular point. This is in fact what historical analysis is all about. It may be that the facts don't change, but our perspective, our place as we look at these things, certainly gives us a new prism through which to evaluate the past. So, why then, are we, at the beginning of this new millennium, turning again to the National Socialist experience? Why study it? Why be involved with it? What's the fascination, the obsession almost, with this terrible period in Western civilization?

The Third Reich was, after all, a morbid, depressing, and terrifying event; a topic, a subject that is certainly not a happy one to revisit. Yet it's a topic that must be addressed; it must be analyzed; we must try to come to terms with it. In many ways, it is the pivotal experience of 20th-century Western civilization, linking political, economic, social, and moral issues that stand at the very core of our experience in the 20th and into the 21st century. In other words, we can't afford not to try and understand what National Socialism meant, where it came from, who supported it and why, and how the regime was able to achieve, or come very close to achieving, its terrifying ideological objectives.

It's obviously more than scholarly problems; this is not an intellectual game to be played by academics or scholars. The balance of power in world politics was fundamentally altered by the Nazi regime, bringing, in the wake of the Second World War, the eclipse and division of Europe and the emergence of the United States and the Soviet Union as superpowers. It has led also, as time has passed, to the European states themselves struggling to find a way to overcome the conflicts that have beset Europe over the centuries, and nationalist ones in particular.

In the process, millions of people lost their lives during the Second World War, either in the war itself or as a result of Nazi terror, a systematic extermination. Fifty-five million people perished during the Second World War, the majority in Europe, as a direct result of Nazi actions. Millions more were forced to flee, found their lives forever altered by the National Socialist regime, and continued to live with the implications of Nazi actions over 50 years after the collapse of the Third Reich. In addition to these powerful factors, there is another that helps to explain the continuing fascination—obsession—with National Socialism, Hitler, and the Third Reich.

Over 55 years have passed since the collapse of the Third Reich, and it's still impossible to pass a magazine rack, a bookshelf, to watch any of the various television stations, without encountering an article, a book, a film, a documentary, a fictional treatment of Hitler, the Third Reich, the Holocaust. Indeed, National Socialism is the most widely researched, discussed, and written about topic of 20th-century history—indeed, in fact, of all of historical scholarship on Western civilization. Why is that? Is it the horror, the deaths, that account for the haunting presence of National Socialism in our psyches?

Certainly there have been, in past years, horrific crimes that run on the same parallel as those ghastly events that would occur between 1933 and 1945 as a result of Nazi actions. The Soviet Union, under Stalin, destroyed millions of lives and sent millions of other people to concentration camps, to the Gulag. Pol Pot, the Khmer Rouge, systematically extinguished a far greater percentage of the Cambodian population than even the Nazis in Europe. Of course, in more recent years, that of the horrific events in Rwanda and Burundi, a form of genocide, has come again to the world stage. Yet none of these events—neither the Stalinists, or the Khmer Rouge experience, and certainly not the Rwandan and Burundi experience—has had the impact that National Socialism has had on our consciousness. Why is that?

The reason in part, I believe, is that, unlike distant Cambodia or the Soviet Union, Germany stood and remains an integral part of our civilization, of Western civilization. It was, after all, the land of Goethe, and Schiller, of Beethoven and Bach; a country which, in the 1920s and 30s, had the highest literacy rate in the world, was one of the most highly developed industrial economies, and stood at the forefront of scientific research and development; a country whose educational system was the envy of the world and a model for much of the American system. The Germans, in other words, were not distant villagers, living in poverty, undereducated, in an underdeveloped economy. They were not desperately poor. They were, in short, a lot like us.

Thus, behind the ongoing interest in the Nazi phenomenon is the haunting question that never goes away: "How could a political movement of such sheer barbarism come to power in such a society? If it could happen there, could it happen elsewhere, in Europe, somewhere in the third world? Could it happen here?" Was there something fundamentally wrong with German political culture? Was it a unique experience, a unique development, peculiar to Germany? Was there something wrong with German historical development that can account for the Nazi phenomenon?

Some analysts have certainly seen this to be the case, have viewed the Third Reich as the logical, and indeed legitimate, culmination of German political development. There are some who'd make the case that the Third Reich is simply the end of a long continuum that one starts at the authoritarian social ethics of Luther, that one moves through Prussian militarism in the 17th and 18th centuries, into the romanticism, anti-Enlightenment thought of the 19th century, into something. National Socialist Germany is the culmination of this development, a deviation, if you will—a deviation from "healthy

Western norms"—France, England, and the United States representing those "healthy Western norms."

In other words, there was a sense in which much of the literature, until fairly recently, about Germany and about the rise of the Nazis and the Third Reich, has dealt with the problem of German deviation. Germany somehow deviated from these healthy Western developments that led to industrialization, a pluralist society, parliamentary democracy. At what point did it jump the track? Was it because of German cultural life, German intellectual life, that tended, the argument often goes, to emphasize romanticism rather than reason, the Enlightenment, and so on? There's the "no Luther, no Hitler" school that I sometimes refer to—that is, that there's a straight and unbroken line from those authoritarian Lutheran social ethics—not religious ethics, but social ethics—down to the oppressive militarism of Prussia, to the horrors of National Socialism.

The first school, the original focus of the deviation was indeed on intellectual developments in Germany. The argument seemed to be that the Enlightenment, with its emphasis on reason that so molded the British, French, and American political systems of the 19th and 20th centuries, somehow didn't cross the Rhine, and that much of German development in the 20th century can be traced to this.

Then, in the 1960s and into the '70s, a new wave of scholarship began that certainly acknowledged some peculiarities in German intellectual and cultural development, but instead tended to emphasize a change in German economic and social development. That is, that industrialization, the argument went, in Germany came late, it came fast, and it was very thorough. That which the British took a century to accomplish, the Germans—and we'll talk about this in more detail in a moment—the Germans accomplished within two generations. That late, fast, and rapid industrialization caused Germany to deviate from a French and a very different English and American model as well, a special German path, *sonderweg* is the German term that's often used.

What we will do at the outset of the course is to talk, not in as much detail as we will about more immediate factors, but we will try to address most of these long-term factors, I would call them, that might help us to form a background for the rise of National Socialism and its popularity. But we also want to look at short-term factors, short-term developments, that would lead, in the course of the 1920s, from Adolf Hitler being an absolutely obscure personality in the lunatic fringes of German politics to within a decade becoming the Chancellor of Germany, from his party being an absolute curiosity that nobody took seriously in 1922 or even into 1923 to becoming the largest political party in Germany by the summer of 1932.

It was, in fact, the most dramatically successful political development in politics, for a party to come out of absolutely nowhere. In 1928, the Nazis got less than 3 percent of the vote; four years, later, it was 38 percent. How did this happen? What sort of people were attracted to National Socialism, we want to ask. There are certainly the true believers, the ideologues, the people who would ultimately be the leaders; people who would, purely for the sake of an idea—I think Americans always have much more trouble than Europeans with the idea of ideological politics, but of course, I think our experiences in the 1990s in this country might change the ways we view that.

We'll look at the true believers, the leadership of the party, the real ideologues, the people who formed Nazi ideas, and the ideas they tried to implement—the folk, the agencies, the forms of government they tried to implement those ideas. But we'll also look at the millions more; the millions of Germans who would ultimately vote for the Nazis, or even join the NSDAP, as the Nazi Party was called (it was a real mouthful). What drew them to this party? What attracted them? What did they think they were getting? Had a whole nation gone mad? I think if one sees often in films and documentaries, there's a use of what I call the dramatic present: "A nation goes mad and is drawn inexorably, almost in a hypnotic state, toward their Führer." Germany did not go mad between 1928 and 1932; we want to look and see what people in Germany in the period, during the rise to power, actually thought the Nazis were. We want to ask who joined, who voted for it, and why.

What role did Nazi ideology play? It's not an obvious matter that if you know the ideas that a party is supposed to stand for, that you've then explained why people voted for them. How important was Nazi ideology? Did Nazi ideology change from 1928 to 1932? In 1928, in fact, the ideology was the same. It found a little echo in German society; four years later, it found a tremendous one. Why? The Nazis would be, as we'll see, the masters of what I would call negative campaigning; they would introduce a whole series of innovations in political campaigning. We want to look at that. We want to look at how the Nazis attempted to mobilize this constituency.

One of the most difficult things we're going to be asked to do, that I'm going to ask you to do, is to forget what you know. Forget the outcome. We'll try to look at the rise of the Nazis the way the inhabitants of Germany might between 1919 and 1933. What did they think? How did they see this? There is no more difficult task in historical scholarship or historical understanding than to remove from your thinking the outcome which you know is on the way, and nothing is more difficult in historical scholarship than to do it in this instance, when looking at Hitler and the Nazis. Nonetheless, that's going to be our task.

We'll then turn, after spending the first half of the course analyzing the rise to power of the Nazis, and now turn our attention to National Socialism in power. How did the Nazis subvert the German government and break political opposition? When the Nazis came into power, they had about a third of the German vote, and Hitler was appointed Chancellor on January 30, 1933. A third of the population, roughly, was in support and voted for the Nazis. In the last three elections in Germany, before Hitler's appointment, the Nazis got about 33 percent of the vote. Another way to put that is two-thirds of the German population might not have been opposed to all the things that Nazis stood for, but given the choice, they chose another political party. So how did a party that really had about a third of the population behind it manage, within six months of 1933, to transform a democratic government—a largely failed democratic government—into a would-be totalitarian state?

What does that mean, totalitarian? That's one of the other subjects we want to talk about, one of the topics that we'll raise, Totalitarian and authoritarian are not the same thing. Nobody thought that the Nazis established a traditional dictatorship. There was something different about this regime, quite different from its predecessors or its contemporaries. This was a regime that ultimately made a claim to the entire person, to the total person. It wasn't simply what you did in public that mattered, it was what you did at home as well; not simply what you said or did, but what you thought, what you said to

©2001 The Teaching Company.

your husband or wife, or your children. The claim was a total claim, eradicating the difference between public and private life.

It was a regime driven by an ideology that believed that it had discovered the key to all human history, and that the movement, the National Socialist movement, found itself at the turning point of all human history. It had to act, or humankind would go in the wrong direction. That meant that whatever was necessary to be done to save humanity from taking the wrong path was justified. If that trampled on traditional morality, too bad. Why was there so little opposition in these first six months or later? Why was there so little resistance, or why was it so ineffective? Mostly, if there was resistance in Germany, why then was it so ineffective?

We also want to look at what day-to-day life was like in the Third Reich if you were not Jewish, if you had not been a Communist; and what it was like if you were Jewish, or if you had a compromising political past. The Nazis made a lot of promises during their rise to power, but what did they actually believe? They made contradictory promises, promising higher prices for produce and livestock for farmers, and lower food prices to workers in the city. Absolutely contradictory, so what did they do? This they could do before they were in power because they didn't have to make tough decisions. But after 1933 they did, so what of all the various things they talked about and promised did they deliver on?

We will examine the real core of Nazi ideology. We'll look at how it manifested itself; how it evolved over the course of time after 1933. One of the things that's very obvious is that the Nazis discovered what I would call an expanding horizon of possibility after 1933, as the opposition that expected a civil war didn't come. So, as time passed, they were then able, I think to their own surprise, to begin to implement the ideology. How do you do that? How does one take ideas or ideological ideas and translate them into actual policy? This is always a problem for any government, and the Nazis discovered it was a problem for them as well.

We'll explore the Nazi determination to acquire *Lebensraum*, or living space, in the east, and to create a racially pure Germanic empire in Central Europe. We will follow the tortured terrible path of Nazi racial policy that would lead from the economic boycotts of Jewish businesses in 1933 to the grisly horrors of Auschwitz. How did that happen? How did so-called Aryan Germans react to the regime's measures, a step-by-step exclusion of Jews from German society, and, ultimately, their transport and extermination? What was known and what wasn't? How did the regime conceal or attempt to conceal—or did it—the ugly truth about their policies from the population?

These are powerful, emotionally charged questions, and examining them is an enriching experience. I've taught this for over 20 years, and it doesn't get easier as time passes. In fact, the emotional demands of examining these questions in depth are daunting. We will try to go beyond the questions of politics and of sociology and pose very fundamental questions. What would you have done? How would you have reacted? Would you have been among those who actually recognized the evil of this movement at a time when it was still possible to do something about it? We all like to think we would; would we? Would we be among those courageous few who were actually able to take steps of resistance against the regime? Would you have had the courage to act?

These are the central issues under consideration in this course, and their relevance transcends National Socialism and it transcends Germany in the 1930s and 40s. They are questions that touch all of us in democratic societies, and are fundamental to our understanding of responsibility, both political and moral, in modern civilization. I said at the very beginning that we wanted to examine both long-term and short-term factors, and so I'd like to turn our attention in this opening lecture in the time we have remaining to the consideration of some of these so-called long-term factors, those factors before 1918 and the end of the Great War, the First World War.

One of the first points of reference that I think we must have is that Germany was a new nation-state. It was the last of the major European states to achieve nation-state status. It was not until 1871 that Germany was unified by Otto von Bismarck, the Chancellor of Prussia. Until 1871, Germany had been divided into dozens of small states—the old Holy Roman Empire of the German nation, which had existed for 900 years when it finally collapsed under Napoleonic pressure—the old Reich, if you will, the First Reich. It was, I can never help saying, as Voltaire pointed out, "neither Holy, Roman nor an Empire." But that's what it certainly was called, and the emperor was in Vienna—Habsburg monarchy.

That old empire collapsed in the first decade of the 19th century, and it was not until 1871 that Bismarck was able to unite Germany into something like a united nation-state. It lacked common traditions; it lacked shared political norms. In fact, "German Central Europe" is the term one ought to use—not "Germany"—until 1871. The question of who or what is German was still a relevant question in 1871 in a way that "Who's French?" was not. When unification came in 1871, it was not the result of some sort of groundswell of grassroots nationalism on the part of the German people. Unification was delivered to Germany by Prussian military might. Bismarck would unify Germany under Prussian auspices through successful wars—against Denmark in 1864; against Austria in 1866, which excluded the Habsburgs, the traditional dynastic family of Germany; and then finally in 1870–71, with the defeat of France—and in the unification without Austria, without territories that had traditionally been seen as part of the old Holy Roman Empire.

A smaller Germany had been created, *Kleindeutschland*, instead of a *Gross Deutschland*, a greater Germany. It was a Germany that had never existed before, and this would be the Second Reich. Nobody called it the Second Reich at the time; nobody started talking about number of empires (*Reich* is the German term for empire) until the Nazis, who of course saw themselves as delivering Germany a Third Reich.

Bismarck, in a way, forced unity on the Germans. There was no agreement. There was controversy about the flag; there was a controversy about any sort of national anthem. They couldn't agree about one. They couldn't agree about the national holiday, like the Fourth of July. They didn't use the day that the empire was established and the Hall of Mirrors at Versailles after the defeat of France, because some of the German states didn't want that. Bavaria in the south wasn't keen on it, for example, and neither were some of the others. So what would they do? What sort of holiday would they take? They looked around with all these different competing traditions from the different states. They finally decided on the day of victory over France. *Sedantag* it was called—the Victory of Sedan—where the Emperor Napoleon III was captured.

Unification had been supported by not so much the proverbial man and woman in the street, but by the commercial and industrial elites of Germany, who certainly wanted to see unification. They couldn't compete with English or French goods, and there was no common currency, weights, or measures and so on. They wanted a united Germany. Bismarck was perfectly happy with the united Germany, as long as it was under Prussian control. His task, as he saw it, was to deliver a Germany that would be based on traditional elites, monarchy, the army, bureaucracy—all supported by the old aristocracy. However, Bismarck was a realistic man in many ways. The age of mass politics had arrived, so the constitution he wrote for this Second Reich was one that had all the trappings of a real democracy: universal male suffrage, long before England, even before France; a Bill of Rights; he believed that the *Reichstag*, the parliament, needed to be consulted.

But without these common traditions, without the shared political past—before Berlin, there had been no capital. What was the capital of Germany before 1871? Nobody really knew. The emperor was always crowned in Frankfurt, but the emperor was Habsburg, off in Vienna. Where was the capital? Nobody knew, so now it goes to Berlin—what had often been seen as a sandbox, a grandiose sandbox of Northern Europe. This new state was beset by three very basic problems, or a set of cleavages or divisions in German society that needed to be confronted.

There was religious division. Germany, after all, is the home of the Protestant Reformation. You have largely a southern Germany that is Catholic; a northern Germany that is Protestant. You have regional division as well. These are old traditional loyalties, and they overlap with religion to a great extent. Finally, there was a social division, a class division, between an increasingly organized working class—industrial, blue-collar, working class—and everybody else. These three cleavages would be the basic areas of conflict that the new German state would confront, added to the fact that Germany was in the midst of this rapid industrialization. Industrialism did come fast. It did come very late, and it was, as we will see, very thorough. This created social tensions that would only be aggravated by the outbreak of the First World War in 1914, and that's what we'll turn our attention to in the second lecture.

Lecture Two
The First World War and Its Legacy

Scope:

This lecture examines the multiple problems of the new democratic government in Germany, especially the legacy of defeat and surrender in the Great War and the hated Treaty of Versailles in 1919.

Outline

I. Before World War I, Germany was wracked by regional, religious, and class divisions, made all the deeper by rapid industrialization.

    A. In Germany, modern values were mixed with traditional ones. The most advanced industrial workers lived side-by-side with artisans belonging to guilds.

    B. In the Ruhr, for example, what had been a glorified sheep pasture was transformed within two generations into the heart of industrial Europe.

II. Otto von Bismarck adopted an expedient for dealing with social divisions. But his strategy for creating a political majority would have a devastating legacy.

    A. The policy of "negative integration" singled out Catholics as a minority—a tactic the Nazis would later revive with the Jews.

    B. Bismarck's policy of persecuting the Church alienated an important minority in Germany.

    C. His anti-Socialist laws rallied many people to the cause of liberals.

    D. Instead of building consensus, then, he established a political environment of confrontation. The Nazis would seek to overcome the political and social divisions left by Bismarck.

III. The impact of World War I and its aftermath on Germany.

    A. The "Great War" was greeted with great fanfare. The Kaiser called for "peace within the castle" to maintain a united front, stirring feelings of national solidarity.

B. But the consequences of the war were deeply destructive.

   1. The war gravely aggravated the already deep divisions in German society. The country was essentially ruled by martial law.

   2. Artisans and farmers felt cheated by inflated prices, and social conflict increased. Over a quarter of a million Germans died in 1916 because of a lack of food.

   3. Germany suffered millions of casualties during the war; only Russia endured greater losses.

   4. German propaganda during the war relentlessly stressed that victory was in the Reich's grasp.

   5. The sudden armistice and defeat left most Germans shocked and dismayed. How had this happened? The army claimed it was betrayed by Jewish liberals and Social Democrats.

   6. The Kaiser abdicated, and a revolution swept the country.

IV. Following the abdication of Kaiser Wilhelm, left and centrist "outsider" political parties created the Weimar Republic. This government signed the hated Treaty of Versailles in 1919.

   A. As a result, the Weimar government was born and lived under a cloud.

   B. The Weimar constitution was progressive. It granted universal suffrage, a bill of rights, a commitment to a welfare state, and a radical system of proportional representation. This led to a proliferation of political parties (more than 35 by 1928).

   C. The government was centrist but tended toward coalitions and short-lived cabinets. It had to deal with threats of recession and severe inflation, as well as other problems.

   D. The postwar period (especially from 1919 to 1924) was plagued by political instability and terror as extreme parties of the left and right vied with centrist parties in power.

Essential Reading:

Kershaw, Ian, *Hitler: 1889–1936 Hubris.*

Childers, Thomas, *The Nazi Voter.*

Supplementary Reading:

Mommsen, Hans, *The Weimar Republic*.

Burleigh, Michael, *The Third Reich*.

Questions to Consider:

1. The Weimar constitution was viewed at the time of its ratification as the most progressive in Europe. Yet, within five years, serious flaws in that constitution emerged. What were they and why were they problematic?

2. How would you evaluate the impact of the First World War on the viability of the new Weimar Republic?

Lecture Two—Transcript
The First World War and Its Legacy

Hello, and welcome to the second lecture in our series on the history of Hitler's empire. We concluded the first lecture by talking about the peculiar social and economic development of Germany and emphasizing the lateness of both German unification and the lateness, speed, and thoroughness of German industrialization at the same time, that—particularly the speedy industrialization—would cause great trouble for Germany, as it proceeded in the years down to the outbreak of the First World War. In this lecture, we want to conclude our discussion of the long-term factors and proceed to talk about really what is the crucial turning point in the development of German political culture in the 20th century, and that was the coming of the First World War and its outcome.

The three cleavages around which German politics were organized were religion (Catholic/Protestant division); region (northern Germany, largely Protestant; southern Germany, largely Catholic, with different areas that were mixed—regional loyalties that remained so profound that in 1871, when the new country was founded, the citizens of Hanover, an independent country that had been absorbed by Prussia and then by the empire, its citizens founded its own party, the Hanoverian Party, unwilling to recognize Berlin. Bavarians kept their embassies in Berlin, and wanted to have a different postal service. So regional loyalty was quite strong; the Hanoverian Party, for example, didn't go out of existence until the Nazis banned it in 1933.) Finally, class division—social division, which is extremely important and in fact constitutes one of the major themes that we want to develop.

Class division, particularly between an emerging German working class (blue collar workers in the factories and the coal mines in particular) and their liberal, conservative, middle-class counterparts—that division would become extremely important because the most obvious domestic political development in Germany before the outbreak of the First World War was the rise of the German Social Democratic Party, the SPD. It was a labor party, its appeal was to blue-collar workers, and it would, as we will see, make enormous strides between 1871 and 1912, the last pre-war election, and end up becoming a major player in German politics. It was the largest party, in fact, by 1912, and after 1890, was a Marxist party, so a party that seemed to represent a domestic threat to the stability of this new German state. More on that later.

The lateness and the speed of German industrialization is also important because within two generations, as we indicated in the first lecture, Germany had caught up with and then would pass Great Britain in many of the areas of industrial production. It was, indeed, the industrial heartland of Europe by the time of the outbreak of the First World War, with rates of growth that were far greater than those in Britain. But the speed of it meant that you had in Germany a very peculiar situation. You had living cheek by jowl, the most advanced industrial workers, organized increasingly into labor unions that would become the model for European labor unions, very modern, living cheek by jowl with artisans, *handwerker*, who still belonged to guilds; the guilds still existed. The guilds didn't go out of existence until 1918–19.

And so you have this very peculiar situation where you have sets of values that are both extremely modern, and those that still represent an older past, that were in conflict. Within two generations, the Ruhr goes from being a glorified sheep pasture in around 1850 to being the industrial center of continental Europe by 1875, and then just continues to grow after that. So, the speed and the lateness meant this conflict of values was there, an older Germany, the Germany of gingerbread houses and black forest toy makers and this kind of thing, is being replaced by the smokestacks of the Krupp works in the Ruhr, or around Berlin, or in Silesia. It meant urbanization; it meant people moving in, certainly from the country into the city, with, again, attendant problems. Urbanization would grow by leaps and bounds during this period, particularly after unification in 1871.

Given the divisiveness of this new German state—nation-states are not naturally occurring phenomena; they have to be constructed, they have to be built. You do have to have a flag. You have to come up with some sort of national anthem. You have to come up with all the things that we think of as almost naturally occurring. They just come, don't they, the Fourth of July and all this? Well, they don't, and this is Bismarck's task. It's not surprising that the song that ultimately became the national anthem, the *Deutschland Lied*, the "German Song," and the verse that we all know, and would come to know in the 20th century with great fear: *Deutschland, Deutschland über alles, über alles in der welt,* "Germany, Germany, above all, above all in the world." Those lyrics actually come from a poem written in the middle of the 19th century that was talking about Germany above Bavaria, Germany above Hanover, Germany above Prussia. It wasn't talking about an expansive Germany; it was unification—to recognize one's Germanness as opposed to one's Bavarianness and so on.

Unification didn't solve this problem; these centuries of division and regional loyalty didn't just go away, and with the threat of the Social Democracy, that had to be dealt with. Bismarck would adopt what proved to be a very successful short-term expedient for dealing with divisions and building some sort of majority for his government, but one which, in the long run, would have a devastating impact on German political culture. That is, Bismarck adopted—he didn't use the term, but historians, I think, have very accurately described it— as negative integration; that is, pick an enemy of the Reich, a *Reichfeind*, and then rally a majority against it. The first of these happened to be the Catholic Church.

From 1873 to the late 1870s, Bismarck conducted a campaign against, not, as he was always careful to point out, not Catholics, but political Catholicism. Well, one third of the population of Germany was Catholic, but what it did was to rally other Germans. Are these German Catholics loyal to Berlin? Are they loyal to Rome? Are they loyal to France, another Catholic state? Are they loyal to Vienna, that's another catholic state? I won't go into the reasons; they are complicated parliamentary reasons that Bismarck needed to alienate the Catholic Party, the Catholic Central Party, as it was called. That's really not so important. For a short-term expedient, he wound up pursing a policy of persecution against the church, which had the opposite effect. It rallied Catholics to the church, of course. It rallied Catholics to the Catholic Center Party, and it alienated an important minority within Germany.

Similarly, in 1878, when that policy had sort of run its course—the Catholic enemy had satisfied him—he needed to somehow alienate the Social Democratic Party. He introduced a series of anti-Socialist laws that would be in effect from 1878 to 1890. What did that do? It rallied support of liberals, conservatives; it also rallied even some Catholics, who now found a way to become part of the majority, as opposed to the isolated minority. But what it also did was to attack— alienate—a growing percentage of the German population: industrial workers, or workers who were drawn to the Social Democratic Party, which at that point was not Marxist, but certainly was seen as being of dubious loyalty (it was internationalist and so on).

As a consequence, I think what you see developing under Bismarck—this is one of his negative contributions to German political life—is that, at a time when German political culture was still new—it was still malleable, it was like clay—instead of fostering a tradition that would try to build consensus, that would build the notion of the loyal opposition, as one had in Great Britain or in the United States—less so, perhaps, in France, where periodic revolution seemed to be part of the culture—at a time when he could have been working to build consensus, he employs this policy of negative integration, in group/out group. If you look at the political pamphlets for Germany in this period, they are confrontational. They are confrontational in a way that even the French can't approach. So, it set a tone that you were either with the government, or you were an enemy of the new state. That style of politics, this confrontational, in-your-face kind of politics, would remain a hallmark of German politics right down to 1933, and overcoming that, ironically, as we will see, was one of the great goals of the Nazis: overcoming class division, overcoming this kind of confrontational division in German political life. That would be the single biggest appeal the Nazis offered between 1920 and 1933, as we will see.

Two trends, then, exist before the outbreak of the war. One was still regional loyalty, the class division in particular, in the sense that Germany was headed toward some sort of trouble, revolution at home. When Bismarck was finally booted out of office, not by the Parliament—they couldn't do it—but by the new emperor, who was about 60 years his junior and didn't want to take any more advice from the old man, Germany embarked upon a new course in the 1890s. He lifted the anti-Socialist laws and—boom—the Social Democrats instantly became the largest party in Germany. In each election between 1890 and 1912, they gained, they gained, they gained, so that they had over 38 percent of the vote in 1912.

There was the threat—the fear, as the international situation heated up and Germany found itself increasingly isolated internationally, heading up to the crisis of 1914—there was the fear that Germany was going to be undermined from within by this Marxist party. In 1890, the Social Democrats showed their thanks to the new emperor for lifting the ban by adopting Marxism as part of its platform. So its policy was to not only bring real democracy to Germany, but also to destroy the capitalist system of Germany. Germany, domestically, then, was a kind of tinderbox before 1914. There were real social tensions underneath the surface.

On the surface, Germany was the most powerful nation in Europe. It certainly had the largest, most powerful, best army. It had the strongest economy. It seemed like a great success, but just beneath the surface of that, these tensions—these social tensions, regional tension and so on—still simmered. There was still a sense that somehow this might be undone. This was the situation when, in the summer of 1914, the war that everybody had anticipated coming for years finally broke over Europe.

Initially, in Germany—we're not going to talk so much about the military developments of the war, but to talk about domestically how it affected German political culture—initially, the war was greeted as it was everywhere, with great fanfare, throwing of flowers at the troops. Everybody believed the boys would be back home by Christmas. In Germany, it also had another meaning, and it was that, finally, the regional, religious, and class divisions of Germany would be overcome. The Kaiser, in a very famous speech, called for what he described as a *burgfrieden*, as "peace within the castle." When the enemy is at the gates, you have to put aside all of your disagreements and pull together to get through this threat. In that same speech, he said, "I do not recognize parties any longer. I recognize only Germans."

For the Kaiser to say this, the emperor to say this, was a definite plea to the Social Democrats, to say, "Look, we accept you in the great political body in Germany. It is now time for you to do your duty while the enemy is at the gates." So there was a feeling of national solidarity as the Social Democrats decided, in fact, to support the war effort. This was not automatic. They were technically a pacifist party; they were technically an internationalist party, but they supported the war effort.

By the end of 1914, certainly by 1916, it was clear that all of the thinking about the war had been an illusion. The war obviously wasn't over by Christmas. The boys weren't back. In fact, in 1915 and then in 1916, the war was going on with no end in sight. Two enormous battles would take place in 1916 that I think marked the end of the 19th century and the beginning of the 20th in many ways. One was the Battle of Verdun, fought between the Germans and the French, that lasted a year. A million people perished in that battle. The British launched an offensive on the Somme later in 1916; 40,000 British troops were killed in one day of fighting, to give you some sense of the scale, and German casualties mounted all the way through 1915 and 1916. There'd been no planning for a long war, so the economy was a shambles.

There was no long-term planning, so skilled workers had been called to the colors early on in the war, or farmers who were necessary to produce food had been called up. Now Germany had to somehow organize itself for a long-term conflict, and that authority was turned over, not to the Parliament, which technically controlled the budget, it was turned over to the army. The army, in fact, established what was in effect martial law during the course of the war. The emperor sort of vanished into the background, and the leadership of the army, Paul von Hindenburg, the first great German hero of the war, and his lieutenant, General Erich Ludendorff, became the real leaders, political and economic, of Germany during the course of the war, and they relied enormously on heavy industry. For heavy industry, if you're going to build cannons and you need millions of boots, you don't turn to small artisans and little handicraft shops to do it. So the army favored big business, as it was called.

On the other hand, what the war effort needed was labor peace. You couldn't have the labor unions going out on strike in war industries, so the army functioned as a kind of go-between between big business and big labor during the war. Indeed, to many, it seemed as if an alliance had been made, with the army functioning as the kind of mediator between big industry and big labor. People who felt on the outside—the small shopkeepers, for example, small producers—in many cases were wiped out. The army had the authority simply to close small, inefficient shops, and it did. About a third of the independent artisans lost their businesses during the war, and their proprietors drafted. Peasants, farmers, also felt cheated. They were called up on to produce—Germany still imported about 20 percent of its food in 1914—they were called on to, somehow, continue this production without nitrates; those were all going for munitions production. They were encouraged to buy new farm equipment, but the government didn't impose limits on prices for business, so plows, all this sort of thing, became more expensive.

In short, there was an awful lot of social conflict during the war. An urban/rural split would develop, with farmers and small shopkeepers believing that the government had simply sold out both to big business and big labor. Small businessmen felt caught in the squeeze. Farmers felt that the workers in the cities were getting away with lower prices for food. Workers in the cities felt that the farmers were gorging, were hiding away their food, selling it on the black market, hoarding their food, their produce, and so on. In 1916, over a quarter of a million Germans died of starvation or diseases related to lack of food. The food just simply wasn't there, and the British blockade was very successful. As a result, in late 1916, the beginning of 1917, the first great wave of strikes broke across Germany, and those strikes would continue off and on sporadically down to the end of the war in 1918.

Meanwhile, official propaganda was producing this really glamorous picture. The war was going well, and indeed, in 1917, things looked, on the outside, very good. Russia was defeated; surrendered. The Bolshevik revolution had occurred—with German help—so that Russia was knocked out of the war, the Germans thought. French and British resolve seemed to be cracking; there were mutinies in the French army in 1917. It looked like Germany might be on the verge of breaking through, and certainly the public was fed this constant diet of good news—any day now, the last victory is within sight; there's light at the end of the tunnel, and all of those images that one uses. But, of course every day, the German population could see the long list of casualties, which mounted and mounted and mounted, and so the price was going to be high no matter what.

Then, of course, the situation wasn't as rosy as it appeared on the surface. The Russian situation was complicated. The Bolshevik Revolution was good; on the one hand it got the Russians out of the war. But the Bolsheviks were determined to spread revolution into Germany, and were sending agents into Germany, trying to proselytize among the German troops, so the Germans had to leave more troops in the east then they wanted to. Germany was also at the end of its resources. It was one thing, as the German commander at Verdun said, "We want to bleed the French white," but Germany didn't have an endless supply of manpower either. And, of course, in 1917, the Americans arrived on the scene. Timing is everything, one is often told, and in this instance, it was perfect. Just at that point when the British and the French found their resolve cracking, the

Americans arrive and just couldn't wait to get to the front and to do their part in the Great War, and provided a real morale boost—I think more important than the actual combat of American troops.

Between March and June 1918, the Germans, with great publicity, launched what was going to be the last battle of the Great War, an offensive that was going to finally puncture enemy lines. Germany would drive into France, capture Paris, and the war would be over. That offensive launched forward, but it quickly ran out of gas, like all the others had done since 1914, and by the late summer Germany's military situation was in a terrible position. The leadership of the army, Hindenburg and Ludendorff, called upon a leader from the Reichstag, a man by the name of Matthias Erzberger, to lead a delegation to go negotiate an armistice with the West.

He was given his orders quite explicitly: "Whatever you do, we have to have an armistice. Whatever it takes, we must have an armistice. Any day now, the Allies are going to break through German lines, and when they do, they'll zoom straight to Berlin." Erzberger went off to negotiate; he was basically given terms for an unconditional surrender. He'd been given his orders—anything it took—and so he signed an armistice. The army instantly said, "That's not what we meant. We didn't mean for you to do that," but in fact, that is exactly what they'd asked him to do, and it meant the end of the war.

To a great many Germans, it seemed as if somehow defeat had been snatched from the jaws of victory—but there it was, it seemed to be there; the newspapers all said so, day in and day out—and now, not only had the offensive not succeeded, the war was over and they'd lost. How? It seemed inexplicable. And then the Kaiser Wilhelm II went into exile in Holland. Woodrow Wilson, the American president, had already given indications he wouldn't negotiate with a representative of the old Reich. And now, a revolution broke out all over Germany. Workers and soldiers, Soviets, councils popped up in all the major cities, and even many of the smaller ones. Workers' and peasants' councils developed out in the countryside. And the government was simply handed over to the leader of the German Social Democratic Party, Friedrich Ebert.

He wasn't prepared for this; the Social Democrats hadn't been involved in anything having to do with the conduct of the war. What it looked like to a great many Germans was that the army had somehow been stabbed in the back. This is, of course, exactly what the army maintained—that just at that moment when they were about to win, the army had been stabbed in the back by a parliamentary coalition of Catholic Center politicians (Erzberger was a Catholic), Jewish liberals, and Social Democrats. Many people didn't believe it, but for the army, it was their way out.

There is no exaggerating the impact of the First World War on German political and social life. Germany suffered almost 2 million dead, over a million missing in action. Only Russia lost more during the First World War. There was hardly any family in Germany that was left untouched, and there was enormous bitterness and disappointment. The social tensions in Germany had grown during the war; in fact, reached revolutionary proportions. The cleavages were greater; the war had sharpened the divisions in German society.

The social lessons of the war, which were learned by many soldiers at the front, were very different. The soldiers at the front had seen a classless society; soldier by soldier, it didn't matter whether you were Protestant or Catholic or Jewish at the front. You were a soldier; you fought for the greater good of Germany. Classes weren't important in the trenches, whether you were a worker or an artisan or a peasant, all were subordinated to the common cause—the egalitarianism of the trenches—and this would be a social ethic that the Nazis would seek to sell to the population between 1920 and 1933 and beyond. In fact, there were a large group of veterans who simply could not demobilize psychologically; the war was all they knew. And one of those soldiers was a young Austrian who'd enlisted in the German army in 1914 by the name of Adolf Hitler.

Certainly in 1919 Hitler was an obscure personality, but he would operate, as we'll see, in an environment of turmoil, trouble, and such crisis that it looked as if the new German state would come apart at the seams. The new German government born out of the revolution of 1918—these workers' and soldiers' councils got together in December and voted to hold a constituent assembly to have a new constitution written, a democratic constitution—but the new republic would be born with this legacy of war and defeat, an association of the armistice with the liberal and Socialist parties, with surrender.

The German republic would be forced to sign the hated Treaty of Versailles that would be drawn up in 1919 in Paris—a document that was reviled by all political parties in Germany; it didn't matter whether you were a Communist on the far left or a conservative on the far right. Germany was forced to accept loss of territory. Alsace and Lorraine went back to France; territories were lost in the east. Germany was forced to pay reparations for all the devastation caused in Belgium and France, and to the British. And, adding insult to injury, a "war guilt clause" was added to the treaty that said that the justification for Germany paying reparations is that Germany alone was responsible for the outbreak of the war—it was a war guilt clause—and the army, Germany's military, was reduced to 100,000 troops.

The new government of the new republic—a constitution was drafted, an extremely progressive constitution. It was drafted in the provincial city of Weimar, safely away from Berlin, where people were still out on the streets, behind barricades, and there was still a lot of revolutionary fighting going on. Weimar was associated with a different Germany—not Prussia, the militarism of Prussia, the authoritarianism of Prussia—but associated with a humanistic tradition in Germany. After all, it was the city of Goethe and Schiller, the two great poets and playwrights of Germany—a more cosmopolitan Germany.

The constitution that it drafted was a remarkably progressive document. It instituted universal suffrage; women were enfranchised in Germany as a result, the first in Europe to have suffrage extended. An extensive Bill of Rights was drawn up. Social commitments of the old empire were continued and vastly expanded. The Weimar Republic, as it came to be known, would be Europe's first welfare state. A radical system of proportional representation was instituted so that there would be, for every 60,000 votes a party got, it got a seat in the Parliament, the Reichstag. Any political view ought to have a chance to have their representation. But this new government would find itself beset from the very beginning with a set of crises from which it didn't look like it would recover.

Political assassinations, of particularly people on the left: Erzberger, who had signed the armistice, was assassinated. Two leaders of the German far left, the Communists, Rosa Luxembourg, Karl Liebknecht, assassinated; Hugo Haase, another leftist politician, assassinated; Walter Rathenau, the foreign minister, assassinated—all by right-wing terrorists. There would be coups from the left and right, and there would be government instability on a large scale. If one were a betting person in 1920, this new republic didn't look like it had much of a chance.

It was in these circumstances that, in 1919, the German army, exercising martial law, would send a young corporal, Adolf Hitler, out to sit in on a political meeting of the German Workers' Party. He would listen to what was said that night at the meeting, and then would join the party, becoming member 555. His background, and the course of the NSDAP in these years, we'll take up in the next lecture.

Lecture Three

The Weimar Republic and the Rise of the Nazi Party

Scope:

We will trace the origins of the NSDAP and Adolf Hitler's emerging role as party leader between 1919 and 1923. Until 1923, the NSDAP was a minor curiosity on the fringes of German politics, but the "Beer Hall Putsch" of that year and Hitler's subsequent trial for treason would bring him and his party national attention for the first time. Convicted and jailed after the abortive coup, Hitler used his incarceration to write his manifesto, *Mein Kampf—My Struggle.*

Outline

I. The Weimar Republic was beset by instability early on.

   A. There were assassinations and coups on the left and right.

   B. There were nine cabinet changes from 1919 to 1923.

   C. In January 1923, French and Belgian armies occupied the industrial heartland of Germany, the Ruhr, claiming that the Germans had failed to make the reparations payments called for at Versailles.

II. Adolf Hitler and the emergence of the NSDAP.

   A. One of many small extremist political groups that arose in post-World War I Germany, the party traced its genesis to the German Workers' Party.

   1. The German name was *Nationalsozialistische Deutsche Arbeiterpartei* (National Socialist German Workers' Party), or NSDAP, originally the DAP.

   2. "Nazi" is a contraction of the first two German words; the term was initially used by opponents to taunt members of the party.

   B. Adolf Hitler quickly emerged as the top attraction of the party.

   1. An Austrian by birth, Hitler served in the German army, receiving the Iron Cross first class, and was in Munich when the war ended.

   2. He was sent by the military authorities to report on the early meetings of the party and quickly joined it.

3. He began his political career as a speaker with remarkable skill. From his earliest political days, he publicly condemned Bolsheviks and Jews.

4. By 1920, he was the undisputed leader of the party.

C. Hitler drafted the party's platform, the "25 Points of 1920," broadening the party's constituency. The Nazis cast a wider net than traditional and larger German political parties. They seemed to offer something for everyone.

   1. Hitler's appearances and the party's activities drew local attention in 1920–1922, but the party was still minuscule and confined mainly to Munich.

   2. Hitler denounced the Treaty of Versailles and outlined an anti-Semitic program under which citizenship would be limited to those of German blood.

D. The crisis events of 1923–1924 gave the Nazis an opportunity to attract national attention.

   1. In November 1923, Hitler and his followers conspired to seize power in Bavaria, then march on Berlin. On November 8, the "Beer Hall Putsch" occurred, and Hitler's plan unraveled.

   2. Yet, in 1924, Hitler turned his trial into a political success, gaining national press coverage of his attacks on various "enemies" of Germany. He was sentenced to five years in prison for high treason. He served one year.

Essential Reading:

Kershaw, Ian, *Hitler: 1889–1936 Hubris.*

Childers, Thomas, *The Nazi Voter.*

Supplementary Reading:

Mommsen, Hans, *The Weimar Republic.*

Burleigh, Michael, *The Third Reich.*

Questions to Consider:

1. From its very founding, the NSDAP was an enigma in the German party system. Why? Was it a party of the left or the right?

2. What was the importance of the Beer Hall Putsch and Hitler's trial?

Lecture Three—Transcript
The Weimar Republic and the Rise of the Nazi Party

Hello, and welcome to our third lecture in the series on the history of Hitler's empire. In this lecture, we're going to continue in our discussion of the political and economic turmoil that beset the early Weimar Republic and examine the emergence of a new political actor on the German stage, and that was the National Socialist Party and Adolf Hitler.

We'd stopped in our last lecture with the observation that this new democratic republic established in the midst of a great turmoil in Germany in 1919 was forced to bear a legacy of war and defeat—a legacy that it did not deserve—and was therefore forced to deal with the problem of legitimacy. For a great deal of the German population, this didn't seem quite like a legitimate government born of revolution, a government now assigned responsibility for the surrender—the inexplicable surrender and defeat of Germany in the Great War, while the military had avoided responsibility, sidestepping its responsibility for the catastrophic end of the war.

Between 1919 and 1923, the new republic would be troubled by a series of economic and political crises, troubles. It was plagued by internal terror, extremist terror. Assassinations abounded, almost always the assassinations of leftist politicians, or politicians associated with the founding of this new republic, by right-wing terrorists. One of the things that the new democratic regime in Germany had not done was to purge the old judiciary, nor had it purged the high command of the army. That failure to purge the judiciary would prove to be quite important for the fate of the Weimar Republic.

In part, the new republican authorities didn't believe that they could afford great instability—that the German population, having suffered this defeat, suffered millions of casualties, now faced by what they saw as a Draconian treaty, allies that were ready to invade Germany if the Germans didn't sign on the dotted line at Versailles—that Germany simply could not afford to have an adventurous domestic situation; that order needed to be restored for the economy to recover and for democracy to have a chance to establish itself. Therefore, Germany couldn't afford to downsize its economy, couldn't afford to suffer unemployment, for example, as the economy moved from a wartime to a peacetime footing.

Therefore, it saw its greatest enemy not as revolution from the right or revolution from the left. The German Social Democrats, the mainstream Social Democrats, moderate for the most part—and I would hasten to say more democratic than Socialist—found in 1919–1920 the greatest threat coming from the radical left, the left wing of the Social Democratic Party that had broken away during the war and would found in January 1919 the German Communist Party. It therefore needed to rely on the army—what was left of the army—to maintain order, and it needed a stable judiciary, and so on. As a consequence, in addition to the problems coming out of these political assassinations, the instability that they brought was the fact that these right-wing thugs that were caught and convicted received slaps on the wrist from the old judiciary as long as the victim was on the radical left or was somebody who was associated—as Matthias Erzberger was—with the armistice, with the surrender, or with the founding of this new democratic German state.

The new republic was also beset by coups from the left and right. The instability didn't stop with political assassination, but between 1919 and 1924, there would be attempts to overthrow this very fragile democratic state by radicals from the left and the right. In January 1919, the Communists in Berlin rose in part to prevent there being an election to the constituent assembly to draw up a constitution. It was brutally repressed by the police, the army, and the new government. In 1920, a year later, a conservative military officer out on what had been the eastern front attempted to overthrow the government and re-establish the monarchy. That attempt was frustrated by the calling of a general strike.

There was also an uprising of the Communists in the Ruhr in 1920, crushed by the army. There was a Rhenish Separatist movement in 1923, when attempts were made to establish a new Rhineland state, an independent Rhineland state. And the French and Belgians invaded Germany, invaded the Rhineland in January of 1923. The French desperately wanted to see the establishment of a new Rhenish republic to weaken the German state. As Poincare once said, "I love Germany so much, I want to see two or three of them." There was a Communist uprising in Hamburg in October of 1923 and then, for our purposes, the most significant, in November of 1923 an uprising of the National Socialist German Workers' Party, the NSDAP, in Munich, that has come to be called the "Beer Hall Putsch."

It's an interesting thing—I've had the occasion to make the observation before that there's no word in English for this. There's either a *coup d'etat* (French) or there's a *putsch*, the German word for coup. But an attempt to throw over the government doesn't seem to have a good word for it in English, and I think there are historical reasons for that. So, in addition to the assassinations, these attempts to overthrow the fragile Weimar government; it's probably not surprising, in this situation, that there was considerable cabinet instability.

After the 1920 elections—the first real elections to the new Parliament—no government could attain a majority. This is part of the reason that this very progressive democratic idea that all parties should have access to representation, that for every 60,000 votes you got, you got a seat in the Reichstag… We can imagine what this means; it means that every splinter group, every glorified lobby, would have a chance to have a seat in the Parliament, and it made coalition-building quite difficult. In this situation, there were nine different cabinet changes between 1919 and 1923, shufflings of the cabinet, and some parties moving in, other parties moving out, and all of the parties tend to be minority coalition governments. What does that mean? It meant that there really wasn't a stable majority in favor of them in the Parliament itself, in the Reichstag, but they would pass legislation on a case-by-case basis, without enjoying a stable coalition government, a stable coalition majority behind them.

It was in this atmosphere of post-war political and social uncertainty and radicalism that the German Workers' Party was founded in Munich. It was founded by a man named Anton Drexler, who headed something called the Executive Committee. The DAP—the *Deutsche Arbeiterpartei*, as the party was called—was really a kind of glorified debating society. It held its meetings in a beer hall in Munich. (I always feel it is necessary to say this: For Americans, it always sounds odd that these big political meetings are held in beer halls; it gives them a kind of atmosphere that I think they don't quite deserve. It would be the equivalent of holding a political meeting in the Ramada Inn or the Holiday Inn, and so on. There were always conference rooms in these large beer halls in Munich.)

In 1919, Anton Drexler had begun this sort of quasi-party. He called it a party, but it really wasn't. It was just a group of guys getting together to complain about the new German government and the revolution. It was only when he decided to have one of these meetings be an open meeting that he had to go and register with the police—the police in this instance being the German army, which was still exercising martial law over Munich, and what would happen would be, the army would then send out someone to observe the proceedings: listen in, write a report—"What did the speakers say? How many people came? Did they like the speech? Who did they seem to be—working class, middle class?"

It was to this meeting that the army sent out a young corporal by the name of Adolf Hitler, who was stationed in Munich at the time. Hitler went to the meeting, as I think we indicated in the previous lecture, listened to the speech, was impressed by it—not impressed by the meeting, certainly not by the organization—but impressed by the speech and thought, "This has possibilities." Within a short amount of time, he joined the DAP, and a political career was born.

There was absolutely nothing in the background of Adolf Hitler to lead one to suspect that this was a man with any special talents or any particular claim on the public's attention. He had been born in 1889 in the town of Braunau am Inn. It's right on the border of Germany and Austria, a point that he thought had great symbolic value later on. His father was Alois Hitler; he was the illegitimate son of a woman named Schicklgruber, and before Adolf's birth, he changed his name to Hitler. It was probably one of the best things that happened to Hitler's political career, since "Hail Schicklgruber" I think would not have had quite the same political clout. There was a good deal of speculation during the Third Reich by enemies of Hitler, and then later, that in fact the father—it was never quite clear who the father was of Alois Schicklgruber—in fact was Jewish, but there's no evidence to substantiate this. A lot of research was done about this, and it seems very unlikely, to say the least.

He had what was a typical sort of Austrian upbringing. His father was a minor bureaucrat in the old Austrian system. He was distant; liked to spend most of his time down at the pub enjoying beer with his fellows—was a distant father. He would come home—Hitler had a younger sister—but he didn't spend very much time with the children, certainly not with Adolf. Hitler himself, Adolf Hitler, formed a very, very strong attachment to his mother, who was everything his father wasn't. She was loving and giving, spent time with him, cultivated his interest in art, and his sister's as well.

Although it would be unfair to call Hitler a mama's boy, with all the connotations that has, he was a person really devoted to his mother. He carried a photograph of his mother with him when he went off to Vienna, when he went in the army, all the way through the war, and the photograph of his mother was still on his desk in the bunker when he committed suicide in 1945.

Her death in 1907 was a great blow to the young Hitler. She had supported him in many ways; she had cultivated his interest in going to Vienna, to the Viennese Academy of Art, and shortly after his mother died he did, in fact, go and attempt to enroll, to be accepted. In a series of competitive examinations, he was not admitted, so in 1907 there were two blows. One was the loss of this doting mother, and then the other. I don't think he'd ever really considered the possibility that his artwork would be turned down at the Academy. If you've seen any of the paintings, you would probably understand why the instructors there thought he probably wasn't the best art student that they could admit. It's significant that one of the things they noted was that he seemed to have trouble drawing people; very good with street scenes and so on, but not people.

While in Vienna, he would adopt the lifestyle of a young artist, and then finally would-be architect, after his art career seemed to have come to an early halt. He spent most of his days hanging around the cafes in Vienna drinking coffee. Hitler was a teetotaler and a vegetarian (a point I delight in pointing out to some of my vegetarian friends). He sat around; there's no indication that he read in any systematic fashion. His reading seems to have been comprised of pamphlets—political agitation of the sort that one could find in Vienna in these pre-World War I days. One of the central themes of Viennese politics in this period was anti-Semitism. It was a hotbed of anti-Semitism, the old Austrian empire, with its Polish population, its Czech population, and into the southeast had a much larger Jewish presence than in Germany proper—and certainly the mayor of Vienna, a man by the name of Karl Lueger, was a major anti-Semite and had organized anti-Semitism in Vienna.

Hitler seems to have been quite impressed with him and with this sort of milieu of anti-Semitism. He developed there, too, characteristics that would be typical of him for the rest of his career: a kind of indolence, this sense of—even though he wasn't an artist, he wanted the lifestyle of one—these bizarre hours, staying up very late, sleeping until noon, going to the cafes. This turns out to be a style of living that he would perpetuate as he was dictator of the Third Reich. We'll talk about that more. The bitterness that he felt about not being accepted at the academy, some have speculated, assumed that the Jews controlled it; the Jews controlled the Academy; the Jews controlled politics there. This wasn't true, but that has hardly stopped bigots. Hitler may have—there's conflicting evidence about this—this really personalized that sense of his own exclusion as part of this larger anti-Semitic worldview that he would adopt. Then in 1914 came the event that would change his life and would have the greatest effect on his political ideas and his future, and that was the outbreak of the war.

There's an extraordinary photograph that Hitler describes in *Mein Kampf*, the book that he write in prison in 1924, of being there in front of the Rathaus in Munich when the declaration of war was read out, and that he was wild with enthusiasm, the happiest day of his life, he said. Sure enough, extraordinarily, a photographer at some point during the Third Reich found a photograph of the crowd, the throng in front of the Rathaus in Munich, and did a blow-up of the photograph, and there in the center is unmistakably Adolf Hitler, waving his hat in the air, absolutely jubilant.

The war would bring Hitler, as he said, the happiest years of his life. For the first time, he felt that he belonged; he was committed; he was involved in a society of peers. His fellows saw him as something of an oddball. He didn't visit the houses of prostitution in France, where he was stationed, as most of them did. He never seemed to receive mail from home, they said. He was a loner, read things—pamphlets and so on—but never seemed to receive mail. He was quiet, and would be furious with them for their going off to be with *French* women of ill repute; he said the nationality was as important as the breach of traditional morality. But he belonged. They saw him as something of an oddball, but still a person that they enjoyed having in the group.

And, in August of 1918, Hitler won the Iron Cross First Class for bravery in action. He was a runner; he carried messages between the trenches. It was a very dangerous job, and in August of 1918, he received this extraordinary thing for anybody, but a corporal in particular. Then in 1918, he was wounded in a mustard gas attack on Ypres and temporarily blinded. He was sent back to a hospital in northern Germany for recovery. He was still blinded at this point, and it was there, while he was recovering, that he heard the announcement that Germany had signed an armistice; that the war was over, and that Germany was defeated. He claimed in the writing of *Mein Kampf* that, then and there, he decided to become a politician.

I think, as so many things in his recollection of his past in *Mein Kampf*, this is something of an exaggeration, but there's no doubt that in that hospital ward, with the news of Germany's defeat and the revolution in Berlin and elsewhere that seemed to be sweeping the old order away, that handing power over to the Marxists, to the Bolsheviks, these two things came together in a very powerful way for him. That sense of camaraderie, that sense of belonging, that sense of the classlessness of the trenches, of all men pulling together regardless of their backgrounds for the greater good of Germany, was a vision that he carried with him from that experience, and would make the centerpiece of much of his political life.

Having recovered, he was transferred to Munich, where he was to be mustered out of the army. Germany was demobilizing, certainly, but there, he was able to stay on the army rolls, and he was given a job as a member of an army surveillance and propaganda unit. His job was to go and listen in to other political meetings and write reports on people and these different parties or organizations that were popping up around. While there, he took courses. The army not only wanted to maintain order, but with the spread of the threat of Bolshevism into Germany, the army wanted to combat that, and so they conducted courses in anti-Bolshevism, things on German history, Bolshevism, the course of the war, and so on, and Hitler went to these courses, where he emerged as an excellent student. In fact, he was selected to go to an instructor's course, where he emerged for the first time as a star orator.

It was at this school for instructors that he realized he could speak. The topic that he chose for most of his talks in this instructor's course was anti-Semitism. "The Jews are our misfortune," he would say, and argued, in the first written document that we have of Hitler's political statement, that "anti-Semitism, based on reason—on facts and not on emotion," was the key. Emotions would produce pogroms, but these things were not very useful; didn't lead to any sort of "final solution." The final aim, he argued, was what he called rational anti-Semitism. The goal of rational anti-Semitism must, and I quote, "unshakably be the removal of Jews altogether." This is in 1919 and 1920, the very beginning of his political career. The "unshakable" is typical Hitler verbiage; everything that he ever said was unshakable. It was *felsenfest*; he was not going to give in; not change a word of it. But this anti-Semitic streak, and this particular statement of it, is very revealing indeed.

It was also there that he would link the revolution that is sweeping away the crowned heads of Germany and leading to what he feared was Bolshevization of Germany. He makes a linkage between Bolsheviks and Jews, and throughout Hitler's career, as we will see, when he spoke, he almost always spoke of what he called Judeo-Bolshevism. It wasn't just Bolshevism; it wasn't just anti-Semitism. It was Judeo-Bolshevism. And Hitler insisted already at this point that his anti-Semitism wasn't the result of religion, the oldest form of anti-Semitism, of course, which had been around for centuries; nor was it a sort of socioeconomic anti-Semitism, accusing the Jews of being parasites and so on. His argument was that, no, this was a racial matter. Jews did what they did, he said, not because of their religion, and not because of any sort of particular socioeconomic history in the past. This was a matter of race, and so for him, a converted Jew is even worse than a practicing religious Jew.

This all begins to come in 1919. Hitler went off to this first meeting of the German Workers' Party. As I said, he was not impressed with what he saw. He found the talk interesting—there were lots of these sort of groups around Munich in this period—but he saw possibilities, and, I might also say, his time on government money, his army paycheck, was going to run out. He was going to be mustered out of the army relatively soon, but he had six to nine months, he thought, still coming, and so he joined this DAP. And unlike the other members of this organization, with the military money coming to him—he had a job, so he had money—he could devote himself entirely to political activity, which he did.

This discovery of his ability to speak would make him the drawing card of this organization. Hitler didn't want it to be a club; he didn't want it to be some sort of debating society. He wanted to take this and use this as the vehicle for the creation of a mass political movement. And his discovery that he could speak—and I think for people who don't speak German, this is particularly difficult to understand. If you see the usual film clips of Hitler speaking and listen to them, the point seems to be, "How many times can I say '*Deutschland*' in the same sentence?" and the shrieking—constantly. His voice sounded odd to Germans, too. It was an Austrian-accented voice.

He had the capacity—some have argued that it was the result of the gassing attack, of the wounds that he'd suffered in his larynx as well as his eyes—but he had the ability to ratchet up from one octave to another so that he shrieks and shrieks. You think his voice is going to break; he's got to stop, he's got to go back down. But instead, it would go up and up and up, creating a sense of crescendo with his speech that everybody found odd and remarkable. Hitler quickly achieved a reputation for himself as a street-corner speaker. He spoke in streetcars in Munich; he spoke on street corners; everywhere that there would be a crowd. And, when the new party began charging admission for people to come to their meetings, Hitler's speaking was one of the things that drew people inside.

There was already a program of this DAP which Hitler wanted to change. He accepted, he adopted what was already there in outline, but wanted to put his own imprint on it. The program of the DAP was drawn up in 1919. It was bellicosely nationalistic: the Treaty of Versailles was a crime; the war had not been Germany's fault—and called for the restoration of German power and prestige. It was radically anti-Semitic, and it was radically anti-Marxist; in fact linking Marxism and Judaism, or Jews, to be more precise. It was also determined to win working-class support for these ideas. This is one of the things that made it stand out. It wasn't just an appeal to middle-class Germans, for whom that program might have had some attraction. He wanted to attract German workers too, to cross the great class lines.

The party rejected the Marxist idea of the dictatorship of the proletariat. This was out; Marxism wasn't what was meant; they meant German socialism. What the DAP and Hitler wanted to do was to create what he called the *volksgemeinschaft*, a "people's community," where class, religion, region would no longer be important. They key was that one was German and a member of this racial community.

Anti-Semitism was linked to economic exploitation; Jews were seen as having benefited from the hard work of Germans. This program that was in shape in 1919, Hitler would take in a 1920 redraft. He changed the name of the party, the NSDAP, the National Socialist German Workers' Party. The name itself was an enigma. National, right-wing; Socialist, left-wing. German, right; workers, left. The very name of the party didn't make any sense to anybody. But that was because they were trying to appeal to a broader population. In 1920, Hitler rewrote the program that became the "25 Points." All the old ideas from the earlier program were there. He called for not only appeal to workers, but also to the German middle class, emphasizing against—still—the anti-Semitism and so on.

For these first two years of the party's existence, Hitler's fame, his notoriety, extended basically to Munich and the outlying areas. By the beginning of 1923, the party had about 6,000 members. It was known around there, but nowhere else. But it would be 1923 and 1924 that would change all that. It would be the hyperinflation of 1923 and then the harsh stabilization of 1924 that would thrust Hitler into the mainstream of German politics. In 1923, in November, an attempt to overthrow by force the Bavarian government in Munich ended in failure. It was an Italian comic opera, with Hitler arrested. But in 1924, as we will see, at his trial Hitler would take what had been a political fiasco, a laughingstock of a coup, a "Beer Hall Putsch," and by his appearance in court, transform that into a major political victory, and establish himself as personality—a peripheral one, but a personality—for the first time on the national political stage.

In our next lecture, we'll take up how the Nazis would manage through 1923, through the breakthrough years of 1928, and into 1932, having made their appearance for the first time on the national scene in this chaotic year of 1923.

Lecture Four
The Twenties and the Great Depression

Scope:

We now examine economic and political developments in the woefully mislabeled "Golden Twenties"—the years 1924 to 1929—and the early part of the Great Depression. We will follow the development of the NSDAP in this period of relative political quiet. During this time, Hitler, released after less than a year in prison, again took leadership of the NSDAP and launched it on a new course of "legality." The party threw its energies into propaganda to win members and participate in elections. Still, the party lacked an issue that would bring it national visibility and, in 1928, with less than 3% of the national vote, the NSDAP remained a minor phenomenon in German political life. This lecture focuses on the pivotal years from 1929 to 1932, during which the NSDAP thrust itself into the mainstream of German politics. Those years of extreme economic crisis gave Hitler and the NSDAP the issues they needed to surge into the national spotlight. Skyrocketing unemployment and a tidal wave of failed businesses became the only issues in German politics. In 1930, the NSDAP's vote jumped from 2.8% to 18%, making it the second largest party in the Reichstag (parliament).

Outline

I. The era of stabilization.

   A. The hyperinflation of 1923 was unprecedented. Stabilizing runaway inflation is always extremely difficult, but the German stabilization of 1924 was a dramatic, if problematic, success.

   B. The United States intervened, and massive loans from the private sector flowed into Germany.

   C. The French left the industrialized Ruhr Valley, which they had occupied as a means to enforce wartime reparations payments.

   D. For the average German, rampant inflation was a nightmare.

II. Following the Beer Hall Putsch and Hitler's confinement, the NSDAP was re-founded in 1925.

A. Hitler claimed leadership of the party after his release from prison.

  1. He was interested in organizational reform and following the "path of legality to power."

  2. He began laying the foundation for a national system of propaganda cells to be controlled and coordinated by the party's new Propaganda Department in Munich.

B. Party strategy lacked an issue during the "Golden Twenties" (1924–1929). As a result, the Nazis were an abysmal failure at the polls.

III. The Great Depression and the polarization of German politics.

  A. With the economic collapse of 1929–1930, Hitler found his issue.

  1. The Great Depression in 1929 brought a stunning drop in industrial production, a sharp increase in unemployment, and a spiraling government deficit.

  2. The latest in a series of coalition governments collapsed in 1930.

  3. Hitler and the NSDAP waged an aggressive campaign in the fall of 1930 and stunned observers by becoming the second largest party in Germany, gaining 18% of the vote.

  B. The economy worsened between September 1930 and summer 1932; consequences included high unemployment, shantytowns, bankruptcies, and growing deficits.

  1. Fearing inflation, the Brüning government reduced state-sponsored benefits and raised taxes, introducing these measures by emergency decree. By 1932, the German public had grown accustomed to the use of emergency decree powers and would not be surprised, therefore, when the Nazis began ruling by non-parliamentary measures in 1933.

  2. The Nazis continued to campaign, even when no national elections were held, dramatically increasing their public visibility.

Essential Reading:

Childers, Thomas, *The Nazi Voter*.

Kershaw, Ian, *Hitler: 1889–1936 Hubris*.

Supplementary Reading:

Mommsen, Hans, *The Weimar Republic*.

Questions to Consider:

1. Why did the Weimar government decide on a policy of inflation, even hyperinflation? What was its effect on German political culture?

2. The stabilization of 1924 was a remarkable economic success yet had negative political ramifications. Why?

3. When Hitler emerged from Landsberg in 1925, he was determined to advance a new strategy for the NSDAP, a strategy that would ultimately bring it to power. What was that strategy, why did Hitler adopt it, and why was it apparently unsuccessful in the so-called "Golden Twenties"?

Lecture Four—Transcript
The Twenties and the Great Depression

In our last lecture, we examined the early years—troubled, turbulent years—of the Weimar Republic, and then turned our attention to the founding of the NSDAP, the National Socialist German Workers' Party and the entry into politics of Adolf Hitler, the leader of that party. In this lecture, our fourth, we're going to examine the emergence of the NSDAP from the wilderness of German politics, the periphery of German politics, into the mainstream, with its dramatic rise between 1923 and 1932.

We'll begin where we had stopped in our previous lecture, by examining events in 1923. Between 1920, when Hitler would rewrite the party program of the DAP, change the name to the NSDAP, and the end of 1922, the NSDAP struggled along. It was a regional phenomenon, popular—or well known, at any rate—in Munich and in the surrounding villages in Bavaria. It was not a national phenomenon by any stretch of the imagination. It was still seen insofar as it had adherence outside of Bavaria as a minor phenomenon on the lunatic fringes of German politics. 1923 would change all of that and begin the dramatic ascent of the NSDAP and Adolf Hitler.

1923 was, at best, a year of chaos for Germany. During the First World War, the German government had inflated the economy. It had paid for the huge expenses of the war effort by consciously inflating the economy. All wartime economies are inflation economies, but when the war ended, France, Britain, the United States, and so on went through a period of readjustment, in which there was a recession, unemployment, and all the things that usually come with this transition from a wartime to a peacetime economy. But the Weimar authorities didn't think they could afford that and as a consequence, continued the wartime policy of inflation. Inflation is, by definition, in the short run at any rate, a progressive policy. There's money to spend on programs. The new Weimar government spent on welfare, on daycare centers, and so on. But in the end, there had to be a reckoning, and in 1923, it came.

During the course of 1921–22, there had been a number of international conferences to try to determine how much in the way of reparations Germany actually owed. The Germans at Versailles had been forced to sign a blank check, recognizing there was an obligation to pay, but not how much. There still was no agreement on this in 1922, and the German government had tried all kinds of things. It didn't want to pay; no German government wanted to pay the reparations. Obfuscating the real value of the mark, paying in kind and then saying it was worth, these deliveries of timber or coal were worth so much. At one point, they even tried to pay the French and the Belgians with paper marks, which the French and Belgians weren't having.

Finally, in January of 1923, the French in particular had had enough. In that month, French and Belgian troops poured into Germany into the Ruhr to occupy the industrial heartland of Germany, to extract reparations from the Germans. The German government responded by issuing a policy of passive resistance. German workers should slow down or simply not work at all, but the German government would pay their salaries through a complicated arrangement. The result was that the German government simply let the printing presses roll, making it impossible to determine, for the French or the Belgians, just exactly how much a mark was worth.

It's difficult to exaggerate the trauma of the great inflation, the Hyperinflation of 1923, as it came to be known. In 1914, if you had a dollar and were standing in the Munich train station, and wanted to buy marks, a dollar would bring you five marks. At the end of the war in 1919, a dollar would bring you 14 Reichmarks; in 1921, 64 Reichmarks. So you can see the inflation creeping up. In January of 1922, a dollar would bring you 191 Reichmarks. But 1923 would see the complete collapse of the German currency. In January, shortly after the French and Belgians invaded, and the German government had declared its policy of passive resistance, a dollar would bring you 17,972 Reichmarks. By August, a dollar would bring you 109,996 Reichmarks. After that, it was impossible to calculate rates of exchange. By November of 1923, a dollar would bring you 4 trillion, 420 billion Reichmarks.

By the autumn of 1923, life in Germany had assumed an absolutely nightmarish quality, a surrealistic quality. A streetcar ticket in Berlin, to go from the center of the western part of the city, around the Kaiser Wilhelm Gedachtniskirche, the Kaiser Wilhelm Memorial Church, over into Alexanderplatz, not far away, was 100,000 marks. A month later, it was 4,500,000 marks. By November, it was 150 million marks. A German hausfrau needed 90 billion marks to buy a kilo of potatoes.

Workers were paid three times a day. You went to work in the morning and were instantly paid. You had to have somebody from your family—your husband, wife, or child—come along to take that money and instantly go out and buy lunch, because if you waited until lunch to use that money to buy it, the money would already be so valueless that it wouldn't buy you a slice of wurst. At lunchtime, a family member came, you gave them the lunchtime money, they went out and bought dinner. At dinner, you were paid one last time, the stock markets closed for the evening, and you were relatively safe until the next morning. Life, as one German glumly observed, was madness, nightmare, desperation, chaos. Shopkeepers didn't want to sell anything; if you sold something today, tomorrow if you took those paper marks to the bank, it would be worth nothing. People were buying things in dollars and pounds sterling.

Big businesses knew how to operate in this. They had access to foreign currency, and contracts called for payment in gold, gold marks and so on. But for the average German, it was a nightmare. In the midst of this economic chaos, the political fabric of the republic began to unravel. There was a Rhenish Separatist movement, sponsored by the French in Cologne, in Achen, in Coblintz. One of the supporters, Konrad Adenauer, who would, after 1945, become the first postwar chancellor of Germany, and finally had his Rhenish republic in the federal republic almost. There were rumors of Communist coups in Saxony and Thuringen where the Communists and Social Democrats were in the government alliance. The government declared martial law, and in fact the army was in charge now of maintaining order.

This situation convinced Hitler that the time was ripe for action. He'd always been wary of making any alliance with the other right-wing organizations around Munich. He wanted his own party; he wanted it to stand out. But now the situation seemed to be right, and he enlisted the NSDAP in a conspiracy—the *kampfbund*, it was called—in early 1923. It was made up of monarchists, right-wing radicals of one sort or another, one group more bizarre than the next—Separatists, Bavarian Separatists—in order to overthrow the government. He enlisted Erich Ludendorff, the great hero of the First World War, who was—I think the social scientific word for

Ludendorff would be crackpot—a great military man, but in politics, was seen as unstable. Hitler took his gamble.

On November 8–9, this coalition of right-wing forces attempted to overthrow the Bavarian government, and then the plan was to march on to "Red Berlin." In fact, they were copying Mussolini's 1922 march on Rome, which had led to Mussolini's establishment in power. But this was a revolution, a coup, a putsch that never got off the ground. The revolutionaries met in Munich in a beer hall overnight. The scene was wild; at one point, in order to restore order, Hitler jumped to the top of a table and fired a pistol into the ceiling to bring order. Finally, around daybreak, the procession began to march down toward the center of Munich, past the Rathaus, down a very narrow street, headed into a large open plaza around the Feldernhalle, where they encountered a barricade. German troops had lined themselves across this open area, and ordered the marchers to halt. Hitler was in the front row, along with General Ludendorff. Ludendorff was there, wearing his World War I dress uniform with his *pickelhaube*, that pointed helmet that was worn in 1914, a chestful of ribbons, assuming, of course, that everyone would know who he was. They did.

When the marchers wouldn't stop, the troops opened fire. A number of the marchers were killed; Hitler miraculously escaped injury. A number of people were wounded and ran away, escaped. Ludendorff marched all the way across the plaza, didn't stop, they didn't shoot him; marched through the barricade and on the other side, the German officer in charge said, *"Herr Feld Marschall,* our apologies," but Ludendorff was taken into protective custody. It was a fiasco; a public relations disaster. It looked ridiculous; this hadn't gotten off the ground; at the first encounter of opposition, the whole thing had come undone. But from that disaster, Hitler would transform it into a political victory.

The trial of the conspirators was to be held in Munich in February and March 1924. Hitler, Ludendorff, and a number of others were tried for high treason, attempting to overthrow the government. The trial was held in Munich. All the others basically pled not guilty. Ludendorff was let off altogether—again, the judiciary not being purged—but Hitler at the trial used it to demonstrate his oratory. "If overthrowing this government of November criminals who stabbed the German army in the back is high treason, I'm guilty. If wanting to restore the majesty of the German Reich is high treason, I'm guilty. If wanting to restore the honor of the German army is high treason, I'm guilty," etc. Even the state prosecutor praised the nationalist motives of Hitler and the NSDAP, and the sentencing in mid April, which was covered by all the journals in Germany—it was a national event.

The sentencing in Munich was a remarkable thing. As I said, Ludendorff and a number of others were actually acquitted. Hitler was convicted; there was no other way, he wouldn't plead not guilty. He was given five years in prison for a conviction for high treason, for attempting to overthrow the legitimate government of the country. And the court expressly held out the probability of early pardon. Hitler was sent to what we would now call a minimum-security facility in Lundsberg, west of Munich, where in his cell he was allowed visitors. In fact, he finally had to protest to the jailers; he said, "Don't let anybody else in." The sycophants of the party would come to see him. He dictated *Mein Kampf—My Struggle*, his political autobiography and political agenda, while in prison. And it was in his years in prison that people in the party began to notice him.

He emerged from prison at the end of 1924; five years had been reduced to less than a year, and already now began to assume this distance; he was now not simply the boss, *der chef*, the chief. He now wanted to be called *der Führer,* the leader. It was, after all, the close party members—Gregor Strasser, who was really the second in command of the party, noticed this—that Hitler after this now distanced himself. He had begun to take on this aura of the mystical leader. The party had been banned in 1924, but under a different name, had run in the elections of May and not done very well at all, and then had done even worse in a later election, because of the factionalism. There were a lot of different chiefs in the NSDAP, and they all clamored to go to Hitler in Lundsberg and say, "What is your position on this?" and Hitler would always sort of agree with the last person he saw. It would be typical of his behavior later on as ruler of the Third Reich, but it cemented his position as the ultimate authority within the party.

In 1925, released from prison, Hitler re-established the party. Again, less than a year after the party had been banned for attempting to overthrow the state, it now re-established itself with the same name;

it reemerges. All it had attempted to do was to destroy the democratic government of Germany—and Hitler was interested in two things above all: organization and propaganda. First of all, he wanted to remain above ideological conflicts. He didn't want to have to decide whether this position was the ideological mainline or that. He was perfectly willing to let his lieutenants battle it out. He preferred to be vague. What he was really interested in was cementing his position as Führer—his recognition as Führer of the party unquestioned.

Organizational reform: Hitler argued that the party had attempted to overthrow the government by force and it didn't work. Now the party had to follow what he called the path of legality to power. "We want to enter the Parliament," he said, "not because we've become Democrats and we believe in parliamentary government. Far from it. We want to enter the Parliament in order to destroy it." The main emphasis of the party ought to be recruiting members and to recruit voters—members, in order to carry out propaganda, and to attract voters. The point wasn't to have a working parliamentary delegation; it was to use this as a propaganda machine.

Hitler had a vision, largely borrowed from the Communists, of establishing a network of propaganda cells all over Germany; that in every town, every village, every city, every city neighborhood, there would be people in charge of propaganda who would be going off to the pubs and to the beauty parlors and to the barber shops, to listen to what people had to say and then to report that back up to the line of command to the Munich headquarters. That way a crude system of survey research would be in place; then the party would know. What they always asked was, "What makes people unhappy? What are the farmers unhappy about? What are civil servants unhappy about? What about white-collar employees?"

There was a lot of dissatisfaction in Germany in this period because, although the inflation had been stabilized in late 1923 within a matter of months—it was a successful stabilization of the economy—the government simply cut off credit, quadrupled interest rates, laid off about 150,000 permanent civil servants, men who thought they had lifetime tenure. About 750,000 white-collar employees, especially in banking—if you don't have all that money to count, you don't need the bankers—were laid off. There was a move for rationalization of industry. It was the period when typewriters were introduced large-scale into German business, instead of having people who had a nice scroll of handwriting; adding machines instead of comptometers; an influx of young girls—not women, but young girls or women—into these jobs as apprentices and laying off older, white-collar employees in particular—men who had a higher salary based on being married and having children and so on.

So there was a lot of dissatisfaction out there. The party attempted this—to create this national network of propaganda sales, to go out and discover opinions so it could then package an appeal—but there were all sorts of problems. The party had no money. It was not a big party; it didn't have financial resources. The lines of communication were not very good; there was no real synchronization of activities. The party had two newspapers, two dailies: a paper in Munich called the *Volkischer Beobachter*, the *Racialist Observer*, and a number of regional weeklies.

In 1928, the party entered a national election for the first time since 1924. The period from 1924 to 1928 in economic terms was one of relative tranquility and relative recovery. The Germans had accepted a financial plan whereby the Americans would invest a huge amount of money in Germany, allowing Germany then to put its economic house in order and then to begin to pay its reparations obligations to France, Belgium, and England. I can never resist saying it was a crazy system, in a way. The United States demanded that England and France, in particular, pay their war debts to the United States, and so what the United States did was to invest in Germany, send short-term loans to Germany on a large-scale basis—not the government, but private investors, this wasn't foreign aid—but with high interest rates in 1924, it made a lot of sense to invest in Germany. So, the Germans, then, would have this capital so they could pay the British and the French, who could then pay the United States. A colleague of mine, who is an international economist, always disputes this with me, but I know I'm right.

Certainly this is the way it played out to the public, so there was a period of relative tranquility. Germany was readmitted to the League of Nations. It had signed a number of international agreements from '24 to '28, not to show that the Treaty of Versailles worked, but to show that it wouldn't. That is, Germany tried not to pay reparations; that hadn't worked, so now Germany was going to make a good-faith effort to pay and then by doing that, would show the allies how impossible it was to do, to pay off reparations. Then this continuous recovery had been made. There was a kind of prosperity; it was the "Golden Twenties," a sort of Roaring Twenties in the United States. But there were problems just beneath the surface. A German political figure named Gustav Stresemann, who was a foreign minister of Germany in this period and really put his stamp on this period of '24–'28, said, just before his untimely death in 1929, "We're living on a volcano. If anything happens and these American short-term loans are withdrawn, pulled back, we're in deep, deep, deep trouble."

In 1928, even with this new emphasis on propaganda, the Nazis were an abysmal failure at the polls; they got 2.6 percent of the vote. A German FBI agent, who had done what Hitler was doing, which was to go out and when he was being an observer of these different political movements for the army, wrote a report in 1928 that said, and I paraphrase very closely, "This is a party that, despite great enthusiasm and energy, is going nowhere. It is unable to attract significant attention or strike any sort of spark in the German population, and is something that basically has no political future." I often wonder what happened to that particular FBI agent who wrote that report.

What the Nazis needed, they believed, was an issue—something that would thrust them into the mainstream. In 1929–1930, one of the leaders of the party, a young man by the name of Joseph Goebbels, who had been in the party around Berlin, became head of Nazi propaganda, and he had his own ideas about what to do. He said, yes, of course, having a national network of propaganda sounds good, but we don't have any money to do it. So what we need to do is to concentrate our resources into something he called "propaganda actions": identify an area that looks like a good prospect for us, and then throw everything we have at it—all the big speakers, all the pamphlets, all the leaflets—make a big splash in a small place, and it'll pay more dividends than these big rallies in cities. What Goebbels was saying is, there's more bang for the buck for propaganda events outside the major cities. If you hold a big event in the Sportz Palast in Berlin, you attract 20,000 people on Monday. Social Democrats attract 20,000 on Tuesday, the Communists 20,000 on Thursday; you haven't done anything. But out in the countryside or in small towns, you'll get a real response. They'll talk about it for days.

The problem was, even with this idea of propaganda, they still didn't have an issue. That issue would be provided by the Great Depression, which hit Germany in great force in 1929–30. The German economy was very closely tied to the American, and when Wall Street collapsed, the German economy followed in tow. There had already been something of an agricultural recession that had gone on through the mid '20s. That was certainly worsened, but when the great crash hit in 1929–30, the effects were devastating. German industrial production dropped by 31 percent between 1928 and 1930. Unemployment catapulted by 200 percent in this period. The government deficit mushroomed. There was unemployment insurance because of progressive Weimar social legislation. As the unemployment figures went up, the deficit did too.

The coalition government that had been in power in Germany through the mid '20s collapsed in 1930. There was a new, moderate government that had come in, a new reshuffling in 1928, and no majority could be created. Policy was turned over; the chancellorship was turned over to Heinrich Brüning, a Catholic Center politician. Brüning, if you've ever seen a photograph of him, was one of these ramrod stiffs. He was the worst nightmare of a schoolmaster. Ramrod stiff, looked like he couldn't bend at the waist, wore a big celluloid collar, and he was one of these people who basically said to the German public, "The only way out of this depression is for us to tighten our belts. We need to balance the budget, we need to cut government expenditures, and that may mean getting rid of unemployment insurance or cutting it way back. It may mean cutting back on these expansive Weimar social welfare programs, and it means we're probably going to have to—there's a threat of layoffs, reduced expenditure—and we're going to have to raise taxes."

Raise taxes in the middle of an economic crisis where there was no bottom? Nobody wanted responsibility for this, and Brüning basically insisted. He said, "Nobody wants to take responsibility for it, but that's what we need, and everybody knows it. All the parties know this is what's necessary," and in fact that was true, but nobody wants the responsibility for doing it. Now, there was a clause in the Weimar constitution, Article 48 in the Weimar constitution, which said in periods or in a moment of grave national crisis, when the security of the society is at risk, the Reich president has the authority to grant to the Chancellor—the real policy maker—emergency decree power.

The president was a kind of figurehead, like the Queen of England, an ersatz monarch. That president in 1930 was the old time war hero Paul von Hindenburg, who had been elected in 1925, a conservative certainly, an old military man certainly, but a man who took his oath of loyalty to the constitution quite seriously. He didn't want to give Brüning an emergency decree power but reluctantly, finally agreed, but in a very, very marginal way. Brüning therefore dissolved the Parliament, and in the fall of 1930, called for new elections. It was a catastrophic mistake on Brüning's part.

While the other parties, all of whom had been responsible for different policies, were in disarray, the middle-class parties in particular—either they had been responsible for the inflation, or the harsh stabilization, or now the Great Depression—the Nazis had never been in power; they weren't responsible for anything. They were in an ideal position. They were associated with no failed policy, and so when they asked people out on the streets, "What do you want?" it never was really "What do you want." It was "What makes you mad? What makes them unhappy?" and they would hammer away at the failures of the other parties. The campaign was run by Goebbels for the first time, exercising centralized control. Membership was rising. The party was able to mobilize all over the country, with coordinated events appealing to farmers, to middle-class voters, to shopkeepers, but also to workers. It was the only party that did this.

It appealed all across the social spectrum. It appealed to Catholics, as well as Protestants. When the dust settled on the elections in mid September, the NSDAP emerged with a vote of 18.3 percent. That doesn't sound like much, especially to American ears, where we have single-member districts and so on. It made the NSDAP the second largest party in Germany, behind only the Social Democrats.

In the aftermath of the 1930 election, the already staggering Weimar Republic was in deep trouble. The success of the NSDAP made a return to any kind of coalition government impossible. Brüning, instead of changing his policies, opted to continue them, and he demanded and received from Hindenburg the use of Article 48. In 1930, Brüning introduced unpopular legislation by emergency decree five times. In 1931, 40 times. And by mid 1932, rule by emergency decree had become the norm; 37 emergency decrees were issued in the first half of 1933, while the Reichstag met fewer and fewer times.

Almost three years before Hitler assumed the reins of power, Brüning had entrusted the German government or the German population to rule by emergency decree, a course that would lead to the end of parliamentary democracy in Germany well before Hitler would take the reins of power.

The Nazis themselves would employ a new strategy—a strategy of perpetual campaigning. They didn't go away between elections, and although 1931 had no national elections, the Nazis continued to campaign as if there were an election going on, appearing everywhere, all over Germany, with dramatic public appearances. Then, 1932 would be a great climactic year of Weimar. There would be elections from the beginning of the year until the end, and at the end, National Socialism was on the verge of power.

Lecture Five
The Nazi Breakthrough

Scope:

The efforts of Chancellor Heinrich Brüning (1930–1932) to stem the tide of bad economic news were spectacularly unsuccessful, and in 1932, new elections were called. Using a revolutionary strategy of perpetual campaigning and other propaganda innovations, the Nazis scored dramatic successes in regional and national elections, emerging in the summer as the largest political party in Germany (with 38% of the vote). Brüning's successor, Franz von Papen, had little support and less success in dealing with the economic problems, and having never been in power, Hitler and his party were perfectly positioned to attack the established parties and their failures. Negative campaigning was raised to new heights. In November 1932, the Nazis suffered an unexpected defeat at the ballot box, seeing their vote drop for the first time since they began their dramatic ascent.

Outline

I. Nazi campaigning in the elections of 1932.

   A. In 1931, the NSDAP briefly took part in an anti-government alliance, giving Hitler access to conservative circles.

   1. The NSDAP's campaigns were now well financed and carefully orchestrated.

   2. In the early spring of 1932, Hitler challenged Hindenburg for the presidency. Although Hitler did not defeat Hindenburg, his public recognition and prestige were increased. The propaganda assault of the Nazis was overwhelming.

   B. In 1932, the Nazis did well in the four major national campaigns.

   1. In that year, Germany experienced two presidential ballots, two Reichstag elections, and regional elections in virtually every state in the Republic.

   2. During these campaigns, street battles between the Communists and Nazis became a plague, as public violence rose to new heights.

C. Chancellor Brüning was unable to strengthen the economy.

    1. Businesses were increasingly unimpressed with his ability to deal with the Depression and to dismantle the Weimar welfare state.

    2. When Brüning suggested settling unemployed workers on East Elbean estates, the Conservatives claimed that he had lost his mind.

    3. President Hindenburg was pressured to dismiss Brüning and finally did so in the spring of 1932.

II. Brüning's replacement was Franz von Papen (of the Catholic Center Party).

    A. What little support Papen enjoyed came from the political right.

    B. He called for Reichstag elections; the Nazis ran the most effective campaign in German history. Although they fell short of a majority (38% of the vote), they won a plurality, which gave them the dominant voice in coalition building.

    C. Negotiations for the post of chancellor now became the issue.

        1. President Hindenburg did not want to appoint Hitler as chancellor.

        2. Hitler would not accept the vice-chancellorship.

    D. The beginning of the end of the Weimar Reichstag ensued.

        1. For the first time since 1919, the Reichstag speaker was not a Social Democrat (Hermann Göring of the NSDAP assumed that post).

        2. Göring engineered the almost immediate dissolution of the Reichstag.

    E. In the aftermath of the July elections, no majority coalition was possible without either the Nazis or the Communists.

        1. Hitler demanded the chancellorship with full emergency decree powers, but Hindenburg refused Hitler and the latter refused to enter the coalition. Hitler wanted all power or nothing.

        2. Papen dissolved the Reichstag, suppressed the Communists and Nazis, and announced his intention of introducing a new authoritarian constitution.

        3. The Reichstag was dissolved and new elections were called for November.

III. The last days of Weimar.

   A. In the elections of November 1932, the Nazi vote dropped—and significantly—for the first time since 1928.

   B. NSDAP was still the largest party, but its constituency seemed to be unraveling.

   C. In regional elections throughout December, the party's vote continued to dwindle.

Essential Reading:

Childers, Thomas, *The Nazi Voter*.

Allen, William Sheridan, *The Nazi Seizure of Power*.

Supplementary Reading:

Mommsen, Hans, *The Weimar Republic*.

Burleigh, Michael, *The Third Reich*.

Questions to Consider:

1. Between 1928 and 1933, the Nazis crafted a social constituency of remarkable diversity. Who voted for the Nazis and why? Who didn't and why?

2. How were the Nazis able to mobilize such massive support in such a short amount of time?

Lecture Five—Transcript
The Nazi Breakthrough

Hello. Welcome to our fifth lecture in the series on the history of Hitler's empire. In our last lecture, we discovered the rise of the National Socialists, discovered the sources of their support, the tactics that they used. In particular, we focused on this revolutionary tactic strategy, if you will, that the Nazis employed, which was perpetual campaigning; that unlike other German parties, they didn't disappear between elections. American parties disappear between elections; who knows where the local Democratic headquarters is, or Republican headquarters is. Most German parties were like that as well, but not the Nazis. They campaigned and campaigned, even when there was no election around. There was no election in 1931— no national election. Still, the Nazis were out in force, constantly campaigning, getting more members.

Members paid dues; the dues were used for propaganda events, and Nazi propaganda was a self-financing operation. It paid for itself; they charged admission, then people came, not necessarily to hear a harangue by Hitler or Goebbels or Gregor Strasser, the second in command of the party, but for an evening of entertainment, where there would be dancing, there would be a band. And at the end of the evening, there would be a speech by a local Nazi and maybe a Nazi speaker. That tactic, perpetual campaigning, would come in handy in 1932, because 1932 would be the decisive year in the sad and turbulent history of the Weimar Republic. It would be in 1932, a year of elections in which the Nazis would finally make that final leap into the mainstream of German political life, and emerge by year's end as the largest political party in Germany.

The Nazis opened the year of 1932 in high spirits. Part of their appeal, part of what they tried to sell to the German population, was the idea of inevitability. There was an inexorable wave carrying the Nazis to power, each election more votes. Whether it was in a tiny state or a local city hall election, a regional election, momentum was the key. There is this inexhaustible energy that is carrying the National Socialist message forward, and carrying Hitler to power. And in 1932, they knew already that there were going to be elections in the two largest German states: in Prussia, which was three-fifths of Germany, in northern Germany, a huge state; and in Bavaria, the most important state in the south, the second largest state, and overwhelmingly a Catholic state. So they were already beginning their preparations to think about those campaigns.

But the biggest decision confronting Hitler, Goebbels, and their advisors was how to approach the prospect of new presidential elections. Paul von Hindenburg, the old field marshal who had been elected president in 1925, was set for a new campaign; there had to be a new election in 1932. Brüning certainly did not want to have the old gentleman have to carry out a campaign, particularly in these circumstances. These campaigns in 1930 and then again, as we'll see, in 1932, were carried out against a backdrop of violence. Storm troopers, the Nazi brown shirts, this sort of militia of the party, would march out into the streets and do battle with the Communists, the Red Front street organization, the Social Democratic street organization. So, to put this 85-year-old man, Paul von Hindenburg, through a campaign in this rowdy set of circumstances seemed to be too much.

Brüning then decided that what he wanted to do was to simply have the Reichstag declare Hindenburg president for life. He thought the old gentleman had served his country well; he was the most respected person in German political life. He seemed to stand above all of the parties, and of course, for Brüning, it made a lot of sense; Hindenburg was the person who had granted him authority to use Article 48, emergency decree power, in order to introduce the very unpopular economic measures that Brüning was using. Brüning canvassed all the parties; they agreed that Hindenburg should stay on. The one he was worried about was the second largest party, and that was the Nazis. Hitler, in quite typical fashion, agreed; Brüning was shocked. He agreed to have Hindenburg simply be declared president for life, no campaign.

But there was a condition; in fact, there were two. One was that Brüning would resign as Chancellor, and that there would be new elections. This was an offer Brüning thought he could refuse, and so there were going to be presidential elections. Were the Nazis going to challenge Hindenburg? It was a real risk; he was the most respected man in German political life. To challenge him would put Hitler's newfound prestige on the line, and how do you conduct a campaign against this venerable war hero? Hitler was afraid, Goebbels was afraid, that they would alienate the conservative voters that they needed. The Nazis were not conservatives; they were radicals, they were revolutionaries. The conservatives in Germany understood this. How do you deal with this conservative old field marshal without alienating them? Nonetheless, in January 1932, Adolf Hitler decided that he would challenge Hindenburg; he would enter the race for the presidency.

The presidential campaigns of 1932 began in February, and the NSDAP was very well prepared. The Nazis launched a massive media blitz unparalleled in German history. Goebbels and his propaganda staff showed what they could do with more money now, with members joining at a great rate. The Nazis were now able to actually do what they had always hoped to do. They held over 30,000 rallies, meetings, and demonstrations. Millions of leaflets were distributed; we're still talking about campaigns that are largely event- and print-driven; that is, radio was not really a factor, there was obviously no television, so it was leaflets, pamphlets. It was meetings; it was these entertainment evenings that the Nazis put on. And Nazi speakers traveled the country from end to end.

The propaganda leadership under Goebbels distributed all sorts of propaganda memoranda to the locals—new slogans for each week, new posters, leaflets—so that the same leaflets, the same themes, leaflets, pamphlets from Koenigsburg out in East Prussia to Aachen in West Germany, would be the same on a given day. It would be the National Socialist Day for artisans, for farmers, for white-collar employees, for civil servants, with all the speakers speaking on the same theme all over the country. Films were distributed, phonograph records, caravans of Nazis with loudspeakers blaring from the backs of trucks, motorcycle convoys through the small towns and villages, all blaring out Nazi messages.

The "storm troopers," the SA, the *Sturmabteilung*, these brown-shirted bullyboys who were the Nazi street organization—their job was basically to protect Nazi speakers and to mix it up with the Communists or anyone else who caused trouble. The SA was absolutely critical in this period; they were the ones who were out there handing out leaflets. They were the ones who were involved in organizing the marches, and so on. The SA in 1932 would have what they called a common *kirchengang*; they all went to church together. This was to allay the fears of Catholic voters, with whom the Nazis had not done very well, that the Nazis really weren't pagans, that it was possible to be a Christian and a Nazi at the same time, all sorts of parades.

The SA would march off into working class neighborhoods in the big cities—in Berlin, Dusseldorf and so on—and hold a demonstration right in the middle of Communist territory or Social Democratic territory. The other parties might talk about fighting against Marxism; the Nazis were trying to demonstrate they really could fight them. They weren't just talking. They were out there challenging the Communists and Socialists for the German worker. The workers had to be rescued from Communism, the Nazis argued.

What one sees in looking at Nazi campaigns in 1932 was an attention to detail. It was something they called *kleinarbeit*, the details of work—little work. What posters worked? What colors were best? Did the posters of Hitler which were straight-on-shot work, or did the profile-shot work best? What sort of images did farmers respond to, did civil servants respond to? And each week they would get their people out in the field to write a report: this poster worked best, this slogan really struck a chord. And so then the propaganda leadership in Munich would send out directives to everyone that said, "This works for civil servants; this works for farmers." The Nazis in 1932 pioneered an election technique and a commercial technique that we have all been forced to live with ever since, and that was direct mailing.

They went through address books. Not every German had a telephone; most did, but not everyone did. But every town, every neighborhood had a thing called an address book, which listed head of household and his occupation. What the Nazis would do is go through these address books, and they would send a direct mailing, written by, let's say, a civil servant, and that direct mailing would go to all civil servants in that town or in that neighborhood. A different Nazi, a farmer, would write a letter that seemed to be a personal letter to all the farmers. It seemed to be an individual; nobody had seen anything like this before.

They didn't care so much about the content. There was no party line to be toed. The Nazis made lots of different appeals. It was like—I always use the image of a wheel with a core—depending on where you stand on the exterior of that wheel, there's a spoke in front of you, or two, or three, and you might like that one; if you didn't like it, you turned it a little bit, and there was something else for you. So if there was some aspect of the propaganda you didn't like, you could turn it a bit, you could focus on that that you did. They tried to offer something for everybody; an appeal to everybody.

In order to win the presidential election, you had to have 50 percent of the vote. At the end of the campaign, there were several candidates running. A Communist candidate ran, a veteran's candidate ran. At the end of that campaign, Hindenburg received 49.6 percent of the vote. What that meant is there had to be a runoff, and the runoff was basically Hitler and Hindenburg; Hitler had received 30 percent. In the runoff, Hitler confronted Hindenburg, and Goebbels and his staff geared up again. They tried to associate Hindenburg with Brüning's ill-fated policies—"if you're happy with Brüning, then vote Hindenburg"—never attacking Hindenburg himself, a great man, a great German, a great field marshal who served his country. But now it's time for a new generation, with all of its emphasis on youth. Most of the Nazi leaders were much younger than most German politicians—Hitler was 42—so this emphasis was what they tried to go with.

And in the campaign's most dramatic stroke, Hitler took to the skies, flying from city to city in an airplane. This had never been done; it was called a *Deutschlandflug*. Most German candidates didn't do what was common in the United States at this time, which was this sort of whistle-stop campaign, going by train, speaking off the back of trains in every town, community, and so on, not done in Germany. This kind of populist sort of approach to politics was very alien to German politics. Not with the Nazis. They were selling populism. Hitler was a *manvonvolk*, a man from the people. So this flight, where he would be all the way out in Koenigsburg in East Prussia in the morning, and then speak in Munich in the afternoon, and then speak in Cologne in the evening—nobody had seen anything like this. The image was that of a peripatetic, all-powerful man who could be all places at all times.

All of his appearances were carefully orchestrated. One of the things the propaganda people always did was to rent a hall that was too small. Never rent a big space, because even if you have a lot of people, if there are empty chairs, it doesn't look good. So they always rented a place that was too small, giving up the biggest auditorium in town for a smaller one. Then they would put loudspeakers on the outside for the standing-room-only crowd that gathered out front. During the course of the day, Nazis from all around would be bussed in to the city—let's say Cologne—so that from all over the Rhineland people would be pouring in to Cologne for Hitler's appearance at 7:00 that night, coming from Stuttgart, let's say, by plane. Then they would have warm-up acts; there would be the local Nazis who would speak, or maybe one of the top Nazi speakers, and then someone would rush into the room.

By this time, there's a huge throng outside. They're hawking photographs; they're hawking autographed photographs of Hitler, phonograph records, little copies of *Mein Kampf*. And then someone would race into the auditorium and announce that the Führer's plane had landed, and that he was making his way to the auditorium. And then 20 minutes, 30 minutes later—he was always late—the crowd being whipped up into a frenzy, then someone would race in and say the Führer's motorcade has arrived out front. More hysteria, and then finally Hitler would make his appearance. The only thing like this that one sees in modern cultural life—that is, not late 20th century; early 21st-century life—is a rock concert. That is exactly the way it worked, with warm-up acts. If they'd had T-shirts with Hitler's pictures on them in those days, they would have sold them, and sold them by the score.

All of this, was, as I said, very carefully orchestrated. Nonetheless, when the final results were in from this runoff, Hitler received 36 percent of the vote. He had not beaten Hindenburg; nobody expected him to. But what he had done was to separate himself from the pack of other anti-system candidates—people unhappy with Weimar. This was a tremendous infusion of prestige for him; he was able to stand on the same stage, in a sense, as the old field marshal, Reich President Hindenburg. At that point, Hitler had become the most visible person in German politics, period; even more than Hindenburg. People who had not taken the Nazis or Hitler seriously began to.

It was at this point, and only at this point, that the Nazis began receiving certain monies from big business, but not much, and not as much as some other parties. The conservatives or one of the liberal parties received actually more. But if you were a businessman in those days and head of a corporation, as sort of insurance policy of giving, you contribute, and the Nazis' anti-Communist stance was quite popular in business circles. Their economic ideas seemed kind of bizarre; nobody quite knew what they were up to. But this was something that business had to be careful about.

But the presidential elections of 1932 were just the beginning. There would be four national campaigns in 1932: the two rounds of the presidential election; there would be a Reichstag campaign in June–July; and then another one in November. And in between, there were elections in every German state so that in April, the Nazis won 36 percent of the vote in Prussia, 32 percent of the vote in Bavaria, 36 percent of the vote in Wuerttemberg, 31 percent of the vote in Hamburg, which until this time had been considered a real Communist stronghold. In short, in a number of smaller states, the Nazis got 48 percent of the vote, and 44 percent of the vote in Hessen. It looked very much like this picture, this image, that the Nazis were trying to create of a dynamic leader, a dynamic movement—there was just a landslide, and trying to stop it was just going against the wheel of history. If you got in the way, you were going to be crushed. The Nazis, indeed, seemed on the verge of something that had never happened in German political life, and that was a majority vote for one party.

Meanwhile, the Brüning government, in the spring of 1932, simply was at wit's end. It couldn't manage; it was no closer to finding a solution to the Depression than it had been at the beginning. All of these extremely unpopular measures—raising taxes, cutting benefits, cutting off unemployment—making this very stern, castor-oil sort of message to the German population—"Tighten your belt, it's time to take this bitter medicine"—it hadn't worked. And worse than that, it had alienated more and more people. It seemed like the Weimar government simply couldn't cope with this issue. And the German economy was in a free-fall. There was no light at the end of the tunnel; every economic indicator was pointing straight down. So the sense at this point was of desperation.

It was a palpable sense of desperation in the streets of Germany, and confrontation, and polarization, with the left gaining strength. The Communists had also picked up support in these regional elections, taking votes away from the moderate Socialists, whereas the Nazis were picking up votes largely from middle-class parties, but with some workers as well. Business leaders were convinced that Brüning had to go. He hadn't been able to undo the Weimar welfare system. And people in the military, particularly General Kurt von Schleicher, who was an influential man in the military and with Hindenburg, couldn't understand why Brüning was unable to make a deal with the Nazis, to bring them on board in some capacity, to tame them, to use them.

Schleicher believed that the time had come to scrap the Weimar constitution and establish an authoritarian regime. He believed that he could use the Nazis—build support with conservatives in the business community, in the military, and in agriculture—use the Nazis to drum up support for this. And using his influence with Hindenburg, Schleicher convinced the field marshal to dump Brüning, who had done so much for Hindenburg over the past few years, and to establish a government above parties, an authoritarian sort of government. He hand picked the man he wanted, and that was a man by the name of Franz von Papen, a man so obscure that even his Catholic Center Party colleagues weren't quite sure exactly who he was.

Papen came out of obscurity. Hindenburg appointed him at Schleicher's suggestion as chancellor. Even the Center Party didn't support him. Papen talked about a government above parties, which was good, because none of the parties supported him. The conservatives were reluctantly drawn to him. His government, his cabinet, was called the Cabinet of Barons because it was filled with bank executives and aristocrats; seven of the members were noblemen and three were industrialists, one a bank director. Papen tried to send signals to business that he really meant business, that he was going to do what Brüning hadn't done—and that was to scrap the Weimar welfare system—and hinted very broadly that what he wanted to do was get rid of parliamentary democracy. After all, it hadn't worked, had it? Who was defending democracy and its effectiveness in Germany in this awful summer of 1932? Virtually nobody. It hadn't worked.

So new elections were called for July 31, 1932. Papen believed that he could win over the Nazis, he believed that he could win conservatives to his side, and it was a miscalculation as great as Brüning's had been back in 1930, when he had called elections. The Nazis tore into the Papen government, attacked it as reactionary— not conservative, reactionary—that it was not what Germany needed, and the NSDAP once again pulled out all the stops, conducted a very ambitious campaign, and when the dust settled on that Sunday in

July, the Nazis emerged with 38 percent of the vote. It had become the largest party in Germany.

And it came close to being what the Nazis always maintained that they were. They were not a class party, like the Communists or the Socialists appealing to working class Germans; nor a bourgeois party like the liberals or the conservatives appealing to just middle-class Germans; or the Catholic Center, appealing to workers and to middle-class Germans, the Catholic workers and Catholic entrepreneurs. The Nazis argued that they had become a true people's party, a *volkspartei*. And it seemed, in fact, that they had. They certainly had gotten votes from not only lower-middle-class Germans. The standard view until very recently of the Nazis had been that they were a party of the lower middle class, this sort of downwardly mobile, undereducated, economically marginal sort of people. In an earlier day, I might have made a reference to Archie Bunker from the *All in the Family* program, but you get the picture. They appealed to farmers as well as to urban dwellers, and they did tremendously well with farmers. They also picked up a considerable vote from blue-collar workers, which no party had done other than the Communists or Socialists before.

They didn't do so well with workers who had been in union industries—heavy industry or coal mining, for example—but they did very well with workers in small shops, workers in small local factories. So in fact, they could make a claim, with a certain amount of credibility, that they were a *volkspartei*, a people's party, an enigma in German politics: something above class, above region, above religion. There were still limits. They still didn't do as well with Catholic voters as they did with Protestants. This was true from the very beginning of the Nazi appearance on the local scene in Munich, all the way down to 1932. Part of the problem was this Nazi association with paganism.

There was a Nazi philosopher named Alfred Rosenberg who wrote an even more unreadable book than *Mein Kampf* called *The Myth of the 20th Century*, in which he laid out the argument that Christianity was really the flip side of the coin of Judaism—that they were both evil, both wrong, and the key was to go back to this ancient Germanic sort of religion. Well, you can imagine how this played with people with any sort of religious conviction at all. So, every Sunday morning—the elections in Germany took place on

Sundays—every Sunday morning when there was an election, every Catholic priest in Germany would stand at the pulpit and say to their parishioners, "It is inconsistent with being a Christian in good standing to vote either Communist or Nazi. If you vote Communist or Nazi, your soul's in peril." Needless to say, this had a dampening effect on Nazi popularity in Catholic areas, and so one of the great goals of the party was to win over the church. In 1932, they had made headway; Catholics were turning more and more to the Nazis, but still not in the numbers the Nazis wanted.

The Nazis were still not doing very well with workers, industrial workers, that had had a social democratic past. And to the Nazis, the '32 elections were disappointments; the July elections were disappointments. They had convinced themselves that this was the last election—that they really were going to get a majority. Everything pointed to it, and even though it was a great achievement in German politics to be now this *volkspartei*, to have 38 percent of the vote—they were the biggest party—it still played badly in Nazi circles. The SA was unhappy; Hitler promised this was the last election. So how were they going to deal with a disaffected SA?

Hitler also came with refused power by Hindenburg. He had an audience with the field marshal; Hindenburg hated him, absolutely despised that little Bohemian corporal, he called Hitler (Hitler wasn't from Bohemia; somehow this got in Hindenburg's mind and it never went away.) Hitler played an all-or-nothing game; he demanded from Hindenburg to be named chancellor. He should have been, in a way; the logic of parliamentary politics would have suggested that. Hindenburg refused because Hitler also wanted to be chancellor with presidential powers; he wanted to have access to Article 48 standing—he didn't want to have a coalition—and Hindenburg refused.

Parliamentary government in Germany had now become a farce. With 38 percent of the new members of the Reichstag Nazis and over 15 percent Communist, the two anti-parliamentary parties had a majority. So when the swearing in of the new Parliament took place, the head of the Reichstag was no longer a Social Democrat—the Speaker of the House, I guess we would call him, who was supposed to gavel the proceedings into order, recognized as chancellor. The majority party or the top vote-getting party always had that position as Speaker of the House, and it had been a Social Democrat. But now, it was now that great parliamentarian Hermann Goering, one of the leaders of the NSDAP.

And Goering, before the Reichstag could even be called into session, recognized a Communist deputy who was shouting from the floor—the whole room was pandemonium—shouting from the floor, wanting to dissolve the Reichstag. And Goering put it to a vote; the Nazis and the Communists voted it out—and so the Parliament, before it had even been in power, was kicked out. Parliamentary government in Germany had become a farce, and everybody knew it. And now there was no hope of any kind of majority without the Communists or without the Nazis.

There were new elections held in November, and in those elections, for the first time, the Nazis' vote suddenly dropped. They had run out of money, they had run out of energy, and it was possible to hold this very complex constituency of supporters together for a while—a protest vote against the failed system, a protest vote against Weimar—but after a while, that appeal runs thin. The Nazis knew that they had a window of opportunity to seize, and they hadn't done it. Their vote dropped to 33 percent—still the largest party, but a real crisis for the Nazis. In a top-secret memorandum drawn up by Joseph Goebbels and his propaganda staff, he said, "We've blown it." He had written in his diary back in March that, "If we don't come to power soon, we're going to win ourselves to death in these elections." And now that looked like exactly what was happening.

The Nazi vote continued to drop in regional elections later in November and in December. It is therefore one of the most bitter and terrifying ironies of all of Western and indeed world history, that at the point when the Nazi constituency was beginning to fray—indeed, to come apart, to unravel—that through a back-door intrigue, Adolf Hitler would be named chancellor on January 30, 1933. That we'll take up next time.

Lecture Six
Hitler's Assumption of Power

Scope:

In the aftermath of the election, party leaders worried that their constituency was beginning to unravel—as, indeed, it was. Yet, at just this moment, in January 1933, Hindenburg would finally appoint Hitler chancellor. That appointment was the result of a "palace intrigue" spearheaded by deposed chancellor Papen. In the second half of the lecture, we will turn our attention to the steps by which the Nazis extended their power over the German state and society. By the summer of 1933, the major potential sources of opposition had been eliminated and the Nazis had established the foundations of a totalitarian regime.

Outline

I. Hitler's ascension.

    A. General Kurt von Schleicher was appointed chancellor in December 1932. Papen stayed on as Hindenburg's private advisor.

        1. Schleicher started a new path of conciliation, hoping to win support from the Social Democrats and Nazis. He did not succeed.

        2. Papen, who despised Schleicher, met secretly with Hitler to discuss plans for a Papen/Hitler government.

    B. The Nazis did well in January 1933 regional elections, and Hitler was won over to the idea of a Hitler/Papen cabinet.

        1. Schleicher requested the dissolution of the Reichstag and the declaration of a state of emergency, which Hindenburg refused.

        2. Schleicher resigned and, on January 30, Hitler became chancellor.

II. Hitler sought to reassure the public that his appointment was not a coup.

    A. The Nazis did not rush to replace people, which created the appearance that they had been contained in a coalition framework.

1. Only three Nazis, including Hitler, held seats in the new cabinet.
2. Frick was made Minister of the Interior, and Goering was named Reich Commissar for Prussia, putting both men in charge of important police units.
3. The storm troopers were deputized as "auxiliary police."
4. Hitler called for new elections.

B. Hitler made a public show of refusing to use the Treasury to fund the party's campaigns. He also made effective use of the radio in his campaign.
1. On February 27, the Reichstag building caught on fire. Hitler claimed that the Communists had started the fire, and in the "Reichstag Fire Decree," ended all civil liberties. This became the "legal" foundation of the Third Reich.
2. Although the election was anything but free, Hitler and the NSDAP still failed to win a majority (44 %) on March 5. However, they were able to form an alliance with the much smaller Conservative Party, and together, this coalition enjoyed a majority in the parliament.
3. Hitler at last banned the Communist Party.

C. Hitler was sworn in as chancellor in March 1933, and called for the passage of an Enabling Act to give him full powers. With the Communists banned, only the Social Democrats voted against it. With its passage, the Weimar Republic was dead, and the Third Reich had begun.
1. In April, the first concentration camp, at Dachau, opened.
2. In May, the regime banned all labor unions and associations.
3. In July, the Nazis outlawed all parties except the NSDAP, thus creating a one-party state.

III. The Nazi consolidation of power.
A. Hitler and his advisors were convinced that the Communists would revolt following his appointment as chancellor. However, the Nazis secured control with surprising ease, and there was no counter-coup.
B. In addition to the Communists, the Nazis had two other important power centers to worry about.

1. Not unexpectedly, there was conflict between the Nazis and the Catholic Church.
2. The German Army worried that it might be absorbed by the SA (the *Sturmabteilung*, "brown shirts" or "storm troopers") led by Ernst Roehm. The SA was the militia of the Nazis, but because of its growing size, it appeared to be the party's private army and, thus, was a potential threat to Hitler, as well as the regular German army.

C. Hitler chose Heinrich Himmler, the head of the SS (*Schutzstaffel*, or "protection staff"), the elite bodyguard unit, to investigate Roehm.
1. Roehm was arrested and executed in June 1934, during the so-called "blood purge" in which Hitler eliminated his rivals.
2. Hitler passed a retroactive law stating that the action was legal and necessary for the defense of the German state (Roehm was said to be planning a coup by the SA).

D. The real winner was the secret police.
1. Himmler (the SS leader) created the SD (*Sicherheitsdienst*, or "security service") in 1931. It was basically an intelligence and internal policing branch of the SS.
2. Hermann Goering created the *Gestapo* (secret state police) in 1933 and merged it with the SS in 1934.
3. The concurrent operations of the Gestapo and the quasi-military SS (virtually a private army for Himmler, not unlike what the SA had been for Roehm) created a police state of unlimited power and ruthless efficiency.

IV. Hitler became president and chancellor.
A. President Hindenburg died on August 2, 1934.
B. The offices of president and chancellor were consolidated, and Hitler assumed them both.
C. He took the title *Führer*, or "leader" (of the Nazi party and of Germany).

Essential Reading:

Abel, Theodore, *Why Hitler Came into Power*.

Childers, Thomas, *The Nazi Voter*.

Supplementary Reading:

Allen, William Sheridan, *The Nazi Seizure of Power*.

Mommsen, Hans, *The Weimar Republic*.

Burleigh, Michael, *The Third Reich*.

Turner, Henry Ashby, Jr., *Hitler's Thirty Days to Power: January 1933*.

Questions to Consider:

1. How would you evaluate Hitler's appointment as chancellor?

2. To what extent was it the reflection of the will of the German people?

3. Discuss the development and use of the *Sturmabteilung* (SA), then the *Schutzstaffel* (SS) and *Geheime Staatspolizei* (Gestapo). In what ways were they similar? How were they different? Why did Hitler decide to choose the army over the SA in 1934?

Lecture Six—Transcript
Hitler's Assumption of Power

Hello. This is our sixth lecture in our series on the history of Hitler's empire. In this lecture, we want to talk about the assumption of power by Hitler in January of 1933 and the extraordinary transformation of a democracy that was certainly in crisis—indeed, had a failed democracy, if you will—the transformation of what was left of the old Weimar Republic into a state with totalitarian aspirations, a process that would take less than a year.

But before we move on to that, I want to close our discussion of the first half of the course with some observations about the National Socialist electorate and how Hitler, in fact, does become chancellor of Germany in 1933. Nothing is more obvious in history—we talked about this at the very outset, saying, "Try to forget what you know"—that no outcome is more obvious than the one that happened as we look back on it. But there is so much contingency (I think is the sophisticated scholarly word that people use now for "luck") involved—being at the right place at the right time, the right confluence of circumstances, which is certainly where Adolf Hitler found himself in 1933.

The Nazis themselves saw their popularity as very tenuous. They realized that they had a hardcore support among certain elements of the German *mittelstand*, or middle class; that was stable. But the others, Goebbels and Hitler realized, the millions who had poured into the party to vote for it—not become members, which required dues and service to the party, but voted—probably the majority of the vote was a crisis-related vote of protest. It was not a commitment to the National Socialist ideology. If support for the NSDAP was a mile wide—we talked about the width of the Nazi support, the *volkspartei* aspects of it—it was also at very many critical points an inch deep. They understood this.

The outcome of the November 1932 elections revealed that Nazi popularity in free elections could not necessarily be maintained at the July 1932 levels. The constituency, they understood, was just too diverse. You could only make contradictory promises to people for so long, or to ask people to vote protest if you're mad at the liberals, if you're mad at the conservatives. They failed, well, why not vote for the Nazis? What could they do? Let them in there and let them shake things up a little bit. How could it be worse? You might get a voter to do that once; you might get him or her to do that twice, maybe even three times. But unless you come into power, unless you're able to change something, then that constituency will have a tendency to decompose. That's exactly what Goebbels meant when he said, in March, "We've got to come to power soon, or we're going to win ourselves to death in these elections."

That's what it looked like had happened. The NSDAP's constituency, as I said, was too diverse, its promises too contradictory, its appeal too negative. The Nazis, as we've repeated over and over again, emphasized negative campaigning—what was wrong with the system, what was wrong with the Weimar system. It was corrupt, it didn't work, it couldn't solve economic problems. It had failed Germany in every way. It held out a positive vision of a classless society, a *volksgemeinschaft*, but that positive view tended to move to the side. In an interview with an American journalist, Gregor Strasser, the second in command of the NSDAP, was asked, "We understand what the NSDAP is against, but what's it for? Americans don't understand this." Strasser, without missing a beat, without turning a hair, said, "We're for the opposite of what exists today."

In the circumstances of 1932, that was a credible response. When other parties would say, "This is crazy. They can't make this work. It doesn't add up; the numbers don't work in their economic recovery plans," and so on, Nazis couldn't care less. Hitler, Goebbels, Strasser, the others, said, "We'll make it work. The will will triumph. This is what's wrong with flabby liberalism and inflexible conservatism, not to mention the Marxists who are beyond the pale. They're too rational. It takes will, and that's what we've got, and we will make this work."

A vote, then, for the NSDAP in 1932 was to a very large extent a protest against a failed system, and not necessarily an endorsement of Nazi ideology. Don't get me wrong about this; there are plenty of people out there who were enthusiastic Nazis and supported the ideas, or what they thought the ideas were, of National Socialism. But these weren't the people that transformed the NSDAP from a small splinter party on the lunatic fringes of German politics; they'd been there all the time. It was the others, the ordinary proverbial man and woman in the street who weren't necessary evil or criminal, who weren't necessarily bad people, who thought, "Well, why not?

©2001 The Teaching Company.

Everything else has failed. What can these guys do that will be worse?"

Contrary to the image of an irresistible political movement being swept into power by grassroots support—the view that Nazis had tried to project—in fact the NSDAP's electoral support was highly unstable, a political compound that was very volatile and that could be maintained, I would argue, for only a limited period of time and under severe economic conditions. This is not simply my view; it's what they thought. Not the Nazi in the street, but what the people who were making the cold, hardheaded calculations in the propaganda department of the NSDAP thought. That secret report that Goebbels and the staff drew up, saying "We've blown it," and Hitler's decision to not go into the government in August when he could have, as a vice-chancellor maybe, concluded with the following lines:

"Above all else, it must not come to a new election"—this was in December of 1932—"it must not come to a new election. The results would be disastrous. But,"—it ends on a high note, as these things always had to—"the reverses of the party can be turned around, and the NSDAP can bounce back, if Adolf Hitler succeeds in making himself the head of a political movement in power, head of the German government."

In December of 1932, nothing looked less likely than that. The party seemed to be coming apart in these regional elections as we indicated. But even if the Nazi constituency was volatile and unstable, even if it was largely a protest vote, there were not many alternatives in December of 1932. In fact, after those elections, Papen was unceremoniously booted out. He had no support, now that the Communists and the Nazis had a majority, and Hindenburg reluctantly turned power over to Papen's Minister of Defense, who was General Kurt von Schleicher. Schleicher believed that he could woo the Nazis, he could bring them into the government somehow, or coax rebellious Nazis away—those who were becoming disillusioned with the party. He believed he could win support among labor unions.

This was a really crazy idea; a military man, a conservative—in fact, a reactionary—winning support from the Social Democratic labor unions? Not likely. That he would be able to woo support away from Hitler, also not very likely. Nonetheless, he pronounced an economic policy that was beyond liberalism and Marxism; in fact, nobody could figure our exactly what it was, and Schleicher was, not surprisingly, unable to generate any sort of enthusiasm in the population at all. By January, it was clear that he had failed in his attempt to form a new government.

Papen had been kicked out of office, virtually pushed out by Schleicher, but he hadn't gone away. He had remained on as an adviser to Hindenburg, for reasons that nobody understands. Hindenburg had taken a real liking to Papen. There have been attempts to try to understand this; nobody really can, and so Papen was a kind of adviser close to Hindenburg. Papen had decided that the thing to do was to intrigue against Schleicher, and to get him out. Papen then, working behind the scenes, engineered a meeting between Hitler and various conservative leaders. Hitler agreed. He was now more malleable; he'd lost the election in November. Hitler agreed to go into a coalition government with Papen. Hitler would supply the rank and file, the popular support, and Papen would supply Hindenburg. He could convince the old gentleman to go along with this. They could not agree who would be chancellor and who would be vice-chancellor, but nonetheless they agreed.

On January 30, 1933, Schleicher was forced to resign, and Papen and Hitler went in for an audience with Hindenburg. They still hadn't agreed about who was going to be chancellor—this is how slapdash it was—and at the last second, in effect, Hitler was saying "I'll take my marbles and go home. I'm chancellor; I'm not going to be vice-chancellor." And Papen agreed. So on January 30, the impossible seemed to have happened; a party that had had less than 3 percent of the vote in the spring of 1928 had now managed to maneuver itself into power.

The appointment of Hitler as chancellor set off wild jubilation among Nazis. A lot of people who had left the party began to return; there was a sense the SA (the storm troopers) thought, "Now the revolution has come. Now is the time we're going to smash this corrupt Weimar system." There were torchlight parades all over Germany by the SA. The cabinet was an interesting one. There were only three Nazis in the new cabinet; Hitler as chancellor (a rather important position) and only two others, Hermann Goering and Wilhelm Frick.

Frick was made Minister of the Interior, and that did not mean caring about trees and preservation of the snail darter; it meant control of the police, the FBI, the political police for Germany as a whole. Hermann Goering was named Reich Commissar for the Ministry of the Interior of Prussia. Prussia, you have to remember, is three-fifths of Germany; it dominates all of northern Germany. That put Hermann Goering in charge of the police in Prussia. So, chancellor and then two positions which gave the Nazis control over the police—critical positions. Papen was vice-chancellor.

Hitler at first certainly didn't want to cause trouble. He was always afraid that something might happen, that Hindenburg would change his mind, so he didn't want anyone to get the impression that a Nazi coup had taken place. So he was sweetness and light in dealing with the members of the new cabinet. He didn't bring about a purge at the local and regional level police offices and so on. In fact, if you read through the contemporary accounts of these early days of this new government—it was called the Government of National Concentration—if CNN had existed or these various other international news organizations, the smart money, the pundits, would be telling us that the real power behind the throne was Papen, not Hitler; that Hitler was "sandbagged," was the term.

They'd gotten him in; he was now going to be the drummer. He would drum up support for this regime, but he was not the man who was calling the shots. That was Papen. Hitler, while being agreeable about virtually everything else, did say he wanted two things. He wanted the Reichstag dissolved, and he wanted new elections. Papen didn't want this because he could already see if there were new elections with Hitler in power, this would be a whole different situation than the November elections, but he gave in. And so new elections were called for March 5, 1933.

Before the campaign could get under way, however, the Nazis used a Communist appeal for a general strike. Everybody was expecting a civil war. The tension in Germany was thick; there was a sense that there almost had to be civil war, with the Communists rising against the Nazis. The Nazis expected it, and indeed, the Communists were stockpiling weapons and so on. It called for a general strike on January 31, the day after Hitler's appointment. Hitler used this as a pretext to have Hindenburg allow him to issue an emergency decree that would go into effect on February 4, for "the protection of the

German people." It permitted a ban on all public meetings, that if the government were brought into contempt, or a ban on any press article or newspaper that brought the government into contempt. Well, if you interpret this, I don't know what a narrow interpretation of that would be, but the one that the Nazis used was that any criticism at all was now an offense, and they could close down newspapers, which they did: Socialist newspapers, Communist newspapers, or moderate newspapers.

On February 5, an emergency decree dissolved all elected bodies in Prussia, and all power was shifted to the new government. This was important because it placed the new government in charge of all judiciary as well as police matters in the state of Prussia. You think, "There's this first emergency decree, then another a day later." Fourteen police chiefs in Prussia were forced to resign and were replaced by Nazis or conservatives, and whole groups of local and regional officials were gradually forced out as a result. The government had, in effect, banned political activity, campaign activity, by the left, whether the Social Democrats or the Communists—their papers were banned—and SA terror against the left now was just given the green light. These SA bully boys, who'd been fighting the Communists and the Social Democrats in the streets for years, now were in effect told it's open season against the Communists.

Then, on the evening of February 27–28, an event occurred which dramatically altered the course of events. In the middle of the night, the Reichstag building in Berlin caught on fire. The large, glass-domed, center section of this enormous building was gutted; flames shot out, the building was really in terrible shape. When the police and fire people got into this building, they couldn't find anybody. The Nazis were absolutely convinced this was it, this was the first shot in the Communist revolution; the Communist uprising had arrived. But the police could only find one person running around in the Reichstag building, smelling heavily of kerosene: a Dutchman named Martinus van der Lubbe, who was mentally deficient. He had some tenuous connection to the Dutch Communist Party, but they couldn't find any to the Communists in Germany.

In the middle of the night, on February 27–28, the Nazis drafted what was called the "Reichstag Fire Decree" for the protection of the people and the state, "to guard against Communist acts of violence endangering the state." The decree basically ended all civil rights guaranteed by the Weimar constitution: freedom of the press; freedom of expression; freedom of association; the secrecy of the mail and the telephone—all now were lost. The government was declaring martial law, in effect, and even beyond that. This Reichstag Fire Decree, drawn up in the middle of the night, would become the constitutional basis for Nazi actions. It gave the government all the authority they needed to destroy their enemies.

The Communists, of course, denied that they had anything to do with the Reichstag fire and said, "It wasn't us. Everybody can see the Nazis set it on fire. Look what they've done. They've come in with this Reichstag Fire Decree. They set the fire, and now they've used this as the pretext to in effect declare martial law." The Nazis flatly denied it, of course. Goering himself was made a special prosecutor, the first one that I know of, to try the case. And even the Nazis couldn't trump up enough evidence against the Communists to link them to it at all. Although it seems highly unlikely, in retrospect, the historical verdict has largely come to be that Martinus van der Lubbe, acting alone, set the Reichstag on fire.

Now, this is not one of those sort of historical mysteries that show up on TV. The importance of it is not so much who set the fire; it's what the Nazis made of it, and that they were able to act like this. They improvised. This would turn out to be a hallmark of Nazi activity all the way through the Third Reich—was improvisation, not acting according to some sort of blueprint for action, but seeing a situation, seeing the potential of a situation, acting. It's not even clear that the Nazis themselves realized, in the middle of the night, February 27–28, what the meaning of all of that was, but they quickly said, "Well, look—this wasn't the beginning of a Communist uprising, but now we have this authority by emergency decree, and we can move against them."

On March 2, 1933, Goering, the chief law enforcement officer of Germany, made his objective quite clear: "It will be my chief objective," he said in public, "to expunge the pestilence of Communism, and all along the line, we are moving on to the attack." The Communists didn't expect that 48 hours after the fire already 2,000 of their top swindlers would be sitting behind bars. "I don't need the Reichstag fire to move against Communism, and I'm not betraying any secret when I say that if it were left to Hitler and me, the perpetrators would already be swaying on the gallows." Then, on the following day, a directive to the police authorities; in that directive, he instructed them to interpret the Reichstag Fire Decree broadly.

The police were to move against the Communists, but "also against those who work with the Communists, or support or further, even indirectly, their criminal goals." In other words, anybody that the police wanted, anybody they thought might be connected, could be arrested for indirectly having furthered these goals. In the days that followed these directives, summary arrests of Communist officials took place, probably about 10,000 in Prussia by March 25; we don't know the exact numbers. Also, Social Democrats were being arrested—not the top leaders, but the mid-level bureaucrats of the party, so that, as Goering once said, "We'll cut them off at the knees." So the head of the party could give orders, but it would never reach the rank and file because that mid-level party activist would be gone. They began to be arrested in great numbers.

In the election of March 5, which occurred two days later, the Nazis were running against a left that was greatly weakened by the arrests and by the harassment of party members and leaders. Yet on March 5 the NSDAP failed to get a majority; it got 44 percent of the vote. In some election and polling places, SA men standing there in their best bully boy fashion, would see a line of people ready to vote, and would simply say, "It's a Sunday, I know you've got plans; you've got other things to do than standing around here. It's taking a long time inside to vote. Is there anybody in this crowd who does not plan to vote for the Government of National Concentration?" Some intrepid souls may have said yes, but they said, "All right, we've counted; you can all leave." Even with that, they didn't get a majority.

The conservatives, a party now associated with Papen, got 8 percent of the vote, and so together, the Nazis and the conservatives had a coalition majority. And following that, Hitler had what he needed; he banned the Communist Party and on March 12 introduced a new flag, actually a black, red, and white one to get rid of the old Weimar flag, the black, red, and gold—or as the Nazis put it, the black, red, and yellow—flag of Weimar. On March 21, 1933, he was sworn in as chancellor in a great ceremony at the Garrison Church in Potsdam. Hindenburg was invited to come, to wear his military uniform from the war; the high command of the German army—not a usual crew for the swearing in of a government—was invited. This was a bow to the army, and this whole business with Hindenburg, to say, "We're really going to restore the old German honor. We're not really radical revolutionaries. We believe in the old values."

In the very famous photograph of Hitler meeting Hindenburg on the steps before being sworn in, Hitler is wearing a top hat and tails. The hat's off, and Hitler is bending down to shake hands with Hindenburg, who looks about eight feet tall in the photograph, wearing his *pickelhaube*, his pointed helmet, standing like this. The photograph—Hitler did it on purpose—it was extremely important. It was to show respect for Hindenburg. And in that speech accepting his position as chancellor, Hitler called for a new law called the Enabling Act, that would give the new Government of National Concentration power to enact legislation for a five-year period (it could have been 20 or 30 for all it mattered, or a one-year period) without having to resort to Article 48, which after all required Hindenburg still to sign off. That Enabling Act was passed on March 21 without the Communist votes in the Reichstag; the party had been banned. Hitler waited until after the election so he could run against them first—the Communist menace—then banned them so that he would have a two-thirds majority in the Reichstag for the passage of this Enabling Act. Once that was in place, the government now had all the authority it needed.

Just a bit before May 1, the Nazis declared May Day to be a national holiday—even the Social Democrats hadn't been able to do this during the Weimar era—to celebrate German labor. That night, the storm troopers moved in and seized union offices all over the country. One of the things that had happened in the meantime was that Goering had said, "We don't have enough manpower and police to deal with all the turmoil on the streets caused by the Communists. We need auxiliary police." Well, where was he going to find auxiliary police? Ah—the SA. So, all over Germany the SA were sworn in as auxiliary police and went about their business. Now, in addition to having their swastika armband on the left arm, they had a white armband on the right to show that they were now the police. The criminals were running the prison.

On July 14, the Nazis introduced a law banning all political parties other than the NSDAP. The police were brought into line under

Heinrich Himmler, head of the SS, who, on his own, without authorization from Hitler, acting completely like a medieval vassal on his own, simply went out to Bavaria, to Baden, to Wuerttemberg and implied that the Führer wanted him to organize police activities in Germany, and surely they didn't have any objection, did they? And since he was known to be part of the inner entourage, local Nazi police officials said, "Of course." And so, Himmler, acting on his own—again, it was improvisation, it wasn't the blueprint—in what would become the central pillar of the Third Reich.

The *Gestapo* would ultimately be brought under Himmler's control. The press, the radio, the schools, the universities, one by one fell to National Socialist control. In a real coup, the NSDAP, the new government of Germany, signed a concordant with the Vatican. This was extremely important. Catholics still remained the largest potential opponents of the regime. In the concordant, the Nazis promised to leave the church alone, not to infiltrate its organizations or ban them, and so on, and in return, the church dropped its ban on the NSDAP.

Only the army and Hindenburg himself remained potential threats to the Nazis by the end of 1933. That threat was removed in the summer of 1934, in June, when Roehm, the head of the SA, was arrested and killed by Hitler's order, and the power of the SA, the storm troopers, was broken. The Nazis, Hitler decided, didn't need the SA anymore. They didn't need the Communists roughed up anymore, the Socialists; they were all sitting in a new institution—a concentration camp—or had fled the country. They didn't need this kind of rowdy organization, this militia. They needed something else. The revolution, Hitler said, was over. They'd won. They had power; they had complete power. Hitler needed the army, which was always nervous about the SA. The SA had over a million members; the army had 100,000. So, for the old army leaders, they wanted the power of the SA broken. Roehm, the head of the SA, always talked about making this a people's army and shoving the old army aside.

Hitler was making a choice. He needed the army; he needed big business, which was also not happy with the SA and their rough talk about social revolution. So this "Night of Long Knives" was greeted in both places. On August 2 in 1934, Hindenburg died. At his death, Hitler assumed the office of president and chancellor, and the army swore an oath of allegiance, not to the constitution—whatever that would have been at this point—but to Adolf Hitler personally. By the summer of 1934, the Nazis had achieved the basis of a totalitarian state, a state that would have a claim on the complete individual. No sources of opposition were out there.

We don't know, but about half a million people had disappeared into prison or into these new institutions—concentration camps—the first of which was opened at Dachau in April of 1933, front page news. The NSDAP, a party with totalitarian aspirations, now had that total control.

Lecture Seven
Racial Policy and the Totalitarian State

Scope:

This lecture examines the consolidation of power by the Nazis following Hitler's appointment as chancellor. During the first year and a half of Nazi rule, the regime was focused primarily on establishing and consolidating its control over German society. By 1935, the racial core of Nazi ideology began to emerge in ever-greater clarity. The main target of Nazi racial fanaticism was the Jewish population of Germany. We will examine the genesis of the racist ideology and the role of anti-Semitism in Nazi thinking. Specifically, we will trace the steps by which Nazi racial theory was translated into policy between 1933 and 1939.

Outline

I. Hitler's regime was one of totalitarian aspirations.
    A. The Nazi system was built on ideology and terror.
        1. The regime claimed total control over the individual; there was no distinction between private and public life.
        2. Yet behind the façade of totalitarian order, Nazi Germany was in many ways a system of organized chaos and institutionalized Darwinism.
    B. The German propaganda machine relentlessly bombarded the public with good news. This barrage was accompanied by the growth of state-imposed terror.
    C. Hitler, as Führer, saw himself as a "big-picture man" and did not interfere with operations of the SS and Gestapo at the regional level. His orders were quite vague. Thus, the functioning of the regime lacked definition of jurisdiction and responsibility.
    D. As viewed from the perspective of the average person, the chaos seemed calculated and social life was organized.
        1. There were no checks and balances or substantive civil rights. Even subjective crimes were punishable, and some laws were made retroactive.
        2. The Gestapo usually made its arrests at night and used other repressive tactics to create fear. Although many

Germans protested the regime, fewer were willing to speak out when it became clear that their families might also be punished.

E. The Nazis used mass rallies and propaganda to build support.
   1. All the news was relentlessly positive.
   2. The newspapers, radio, and newsreels spewed forth a steady stream of propaganda, emphasizing the positive achievements of the regime.
   3. No dissenting opinions could be heard. The official view of Nazi society was one of happy farmers, workers, and middle-class Germans working together in a classless society—a *Volksgemeinschaft*, or people's community. Hitler was celebrated as a man of the people.

II. Evolution of Nazi racial policy.
   A. Anti-Semitism was a central aspect of the Nazi program.
      1. In *Mein Kampf*, Hitler propounded his theories about the inferiority of the Jews (and other non-Aryans) and their corruption of German society.
      2. Before 1933, the Nazis subtly linked anti-Semitism to other issues, especially economic ones.
      3. With the onset of the Depression, the Nazis, while still presenting their anti-Semitic positions, tended to emphasize other aspects of their program in their public appeals.
      4. Following their rise to power, they could pursue anti-Semitism more openly.

   B. After 1933, Nazi racial policy proceeded in three phases.
      1. The period from 1933 to 1935 was one of early "legal" discrimination against the Jews in the civil service and the professions—law, medicine, and education.
      2. The years 1935 to 1938 were characterized by the passage of the Nürnberg (Nuremberg) Laws in 1935; Nazi policy in these years focused on *Entjüdung*, pressuring Jews to leave Germany.
      3. The infamous *Reichskristallnacht* in November 1938, the first nation-wide coordinated act of violence against the Jewish community, marked a new and sinister phase of Nazi actions.

4. The Second World War would usher in the last and most devastating phase of Nazi racial policy, the "final solution to the Jewish question," meaning mass murder.

III. The evolution of Nazi Jewish policy.

A. Complicated bureaucratic politics played as much a role in the decision to exterminate the Jews as did Nazi ideology.

B. After a burst of anti-Semitic measures in 1933, the national regime seemed to lose interest in new initiatives against the Jews.

   1. Jewish businesses were boycotted in 1933.

   2. Legislation was enacted in April 1933 to eliminate Jews from the civil service. After being chastised by Hindenburg, the Nazis chose not to ostracize Jewish veterans.

   3. A terrible irony was that, until this time, Germany was considered a haven for Eastern European Jews.

   4. Regional and local Nazi activists took actions against Jews in what were called *Einzelaktionen*, or "individual actions."

C. The repression entered a new phase between 1935 and 1938.

   1. The Nürnberg Laws of 1935 deprived Jews of their civil rights; Jews were denied German citizenship, intermarriage between Germans and Jews was prohibited, and Jews were barred from certain professions. The laws were made retroactive.

   2. The regime attempted to define systematically who was or was not a Jew. Hitler refused to take a position, typical of his determination not to make clear decisions or take sides in internal party disputes.

   3. Still, after the Nürnberg Laws, no new measures would be undertaken until 1938.

D. The regime carried out additional steps between 1938 and 1941.

   1. The first act of mass violence against the Jewish community to be clearly orchestrated by the government was the *Kristallnacht* (or "Night of Broken Glass") on November 10, 1938.

   2. Many Jews were killed or injured, and their property and synagogues were damaged or destroyed.

Essential Reading:

Arendt, Hannah, *Totalitarianism*.

Burleigh, Michael, *The Third Reich*.

Hitler, Adolf, *Mein Kampf* (focus on the chapters addressing the Jews and other "undesirables" and his concepts of racial purity).

Friedländer, Saul, *Nazi Germany and the Jews*.

Supplementary Reading:

Kershaw, Ian, *Hitler: 1889–1936 Hubris*.

Peukart, Detlev, *Inside Nazi Germany*.

Gellately, Robert, *The Gestapo and German Society*.

Kaplan, Marion, *Between Dignity and Despair*.

Klemperer, Viktor, *I Will Bear Witness, 1933–1941*.

Questions to Consider:

1. What is totalitarianism? How is it different from authoritarian dictatorships, such as Mussolini's Italy or Franco's Spain?

2. Trace the history of anti-Jewish laws in Germany following Hitler's assumption of power. What was the international reaction to the Nuremberg Laws and *Kristallnacht*?

3. Were the Nazis acting according to some sort of blueprint as they introduced their anti-Jewish measures step-by-step, or did circumstance, improvisation, and the peculiar decision-making style of the Third Reich play a significant role?

Lecture Seven—Transcript
Racial Policy and the Totalitarian State

Hello, and welcome to the seventh in our lectures on the history of Hitler's empire. We had stopped in our last lecture with the establishment of the National Socialist dictatorship, Hitler's assumption of power, and the bringing into line of German society. We had seen how, by the end of 1933, the party had already achieved virtually total power. By the end of 1934, the last restraints—the army, the presence of Reich President Hindenburg—had also been removed, so that the Nazis now stood on the verge of being able to realize whatever plans they might have, the unfolding of their ideology. Indeed, for the first year or so of the National Socialist reign, their concentration was focused on seizing and then consolidating power.

It would only be gradually, but certainly after the summer of 1934, that the real core of National Socialist ideology would emerge in increasingly crystalline fashion, particularly with regard to racial policy, and it is about racial policy that I want to speak in this lecture. But before turning to that, I want to talk a little bit about totalitarianism and the nature of the society in which these racial policies unfolded. One of the most difficult things to do in historical analysis—I think we may have referred to it—is to keep the simultaneity of events in front of you, that successes in foreign policy often, as we will see, correspond to some of the ugliest aspects of Nazi racial policy. So these things have to be calibrated so that one understands how something that one would think would draw enormous public attention could, in some ways, be swept to the side, while greater attention was focused on great foreign policy victories, let's say.

And there's something else that I think needs to be emphasized about this society in which these racial policies would emerge, and that is the nature of what totalitarianism was. It wasn't simply, as we've said before, a regime with a claim to the total person, a regime which wants to efface the distinction between public and private life. It is also a regime that has an ideology and believes that it's discovered the key to all human history—a key to the past, the present, and a guide for the future. In the case of the Soviet Union under Stalin, which one could also make the case for being a regime of totalitarian aspirations, they believed that the dialectical materialism was the key; class struggle was the key to the dynamics of all human history.

For the Nazis, it would become clear in the course of the 1930s that it was race that was the key to understanding human history. The Nazis would attempt to take a racial ideology and translate that into policy. This is not an obvious thing, how one takes ideas, ideology and translates them into policy, and that's something we want to address. So the regime, with its claim to the total person, and having an ideology in which it believes so fanatically, that the whole system of morality is shifted—anything that will keep the party, the movement, the state, on the historical straight and narrow is morally just. And if that means breaking all sorts of rules, then so be it. If it means going against traditional Judeo-Christian morality, okay. These extraordinary goals require extraordinary measures.

At the same time that this ideology is becoming increasingly clear, the system would work also, in terms of its ideological goals, with propaganda—hammering away in a positive sense about the regime. What's it doing? What's it doing for Germany in addition to these larger ideological goals? Constantly hammering away at good news about what the new regime has done. There's no such thing as bad news reported in the press, not in this sort of regime. And if the relentless positive propaganda is not enough, there's always the system of terror that would be unleashed between 1933 and 1945.

The SS, the *Gestapo*, the state secret police would be given authority to ferret out enemies of the state and of the party wherever they might exist, and to take extraordinary measures against them. Indeed, the concentration camps to which we alluded with the establishment of Dachau in 1933, those camps in Germany were used for German political prisoners in the period before the war. The *Gestapo* got this down to a science, discovering that the best time to arrest people was in the middle of the night, between 2:00 and 3:00 in the morning, to be quite exact. You would go—people were more vulnerable then— go knock on the door, go in, take the person out.

This served several purposes. It made the victim more vulnerable to take him down to the *Gestapo* headquarters for questioning, but also the neighbors didn't really quite see it. They might hear it, out in the hallway, in the apartment building, so that the next morning they said, "Did you hear that? I think Frau Schmidt had a visitor last night. This was not a romantic call; men in leather coats. I wonder what's going on. Maybe Frau Schmidt is not reliable." People became more cautious; didn't speak to one another as much about this sort of thing. The *Gestapo* also found that people were more than willing to inform on their neighbors. If you had a grudge against a neighbor whose dog barked all through the night, and you complained to the neighbor many times, but it didn't work and they didn't do anything, you might make an anonymous phone call to Gestapo headquarters in your town or village. That person would be dragged in for questioning about unsocial behavior. It wouldn't be a dog barking; but something else.

They also discovered that there were brave people who were willing to take a risk, people willing to throw their lives away to express their opposition to the regime. Of course, if you do something, an act of opposition, and it's not reported in the press, it's not on the radio, what does it do? But there were people who would do that, who were that courageous—lots of them. But the Nazis also introduced something called *sippenhaft*, which meant that not only would they arrest you, but your husband, your children, parents, possibly other relatives, possibly other friends. They knew that, although there were very many brave people who were willing to give their lives away, there weren't quite so many people who were willing to see their children consigned to a concentration camp, or their husband or wife, or parents.

So, this system of terror was always in place. Then there was also the ideology—the relentless good news to balance the uglier features of the regime. The Third Reich was constantly drumming on this good news, and the enthusiasm of the population. Everybody was behind the regime; there was no opposition expressed. So, if you had opposition, if you had doubts, if you had questions, who did you get to talk to them about? You couldn't write a letter to the editor. If you went with friends, people you'd known all your life, you'd sit down and suddenly discover that people are a little warier about saying things.

You might tell a joke one day. There were lots of jokes in the Third Reich, *flüsterte witze*, they were called, whispered jokes, a joke about racial policy that says, "Yes, I'm an Aryan, I'm a blond like Hitler, I'm tall like Goebbels"—who was about 5'5"—"and slender like Goering"—who must have weighed about 275 pounds later on in his life. You might tell this joke at the pub one night. Everyone would laugh, and then you might tell it at another pub two days later. And everybody would laugh. That night, there would be a knock on the door, and it would be the Gestapo.

Uncertainty, confusion—people were left with no fixed points of orientation. There was no reality in Germany; there was not National Socialist reality. If you were opposed to some aspect of the regime's policy, and nobody else seemed to be—you couldn't read about it anywhere, you couldn't see it anywhere, you couldn't talk to friends about it—maybe it's you who's out of step. Maybe you're being an alarmist. There was a very famous quote by a German clergyman, who said, "At first they went after the Communists, and I was not a Communist, so I did nothing. Then they went after the Socialists, and I was a little uneasier, but I wasn't a Socialist, and so I did nothing. Then they went after the church, and I was a churchman, but then it was too late."

Little by little—the Nazis called it salami tactics—you don't stop at Step A, why stop at Step B. If you don't cause trouble in Step C, why not D, until you finally find yourself corrupted by the regime and compromised by it. As one person said, it was like a farmer watching corn grow in his field. You don't notice it at all day to day; you're busy doing your own job, keeping your nose clean, keeping out of trouble, pursuing your career, worrying about your kids' education, etc. But then suddenly the farmer looks around, and the corn is over his head. This is the way it was for a great many people in Germany. All around, the good news. The media was dominated by the Nazis, and there were all these Nazi activities: the great national celebration for the Führer's birthday on April 20; the Beer Hall Putsch was celebrated as if it had been a great historic event for the Nazis, every year. The party rally in September, which was like a big convention that went on for a week, was obviously the high point of the Nazi calendar, with great fanfare.

Social life was now organized. Boys were introduced into the Hitler Youth, girls into the *Bund Deutscher Madel*, the League of German Girls, women into the National Socialist Women's Organization, the National Socialist Student League, the National Socialist Teachers' League, the National Socialist Attorneys' Organization, the National Socialist Physicians' League—you get the picture. All had their own special badges, their own flags, slogans, and so on. My favorite one is "Barbers, too, face great tasks." This positive imagery over and over again, also of Hitler the populist, Hitler with a spade out in the opening of the big Autobahn, the big superhighways that were introduced. Hitler at the Harvest Festival; he was a man of the people. Who could be opposed to this?

There was no trouble on the streets anymore. The Communists were gone; there weren't pitched battles anymore. The unemployed would slowly disappear from the streets because they would be drafted into something called the Labor Front, given uniforms and shovels, which they handled with a Manual of Arms like a weapon in the army. All of this created an environment in which the National Socialists could introduce other policies which would be much more controversial, and the most obvious one would be racial policy.

It was racial policy—of all the things the Nazis had talked about before 1933, of all the different aspects of Nazi ideology, Nazi campaign promises, Nazi social promises—anti-Semitism had been one of the various threads in Nazi appeal. No one could have had any doubt about Nazi fanatical anti-Semitism. This was up front, obvious; it was, in so many ways, the essence of National Socialism—and yet, I think an aspect of the party's propaganda that people took less seriously than they did the appeals on the social and economic issues and on this negative campaigning, the anti-system aspect of the party's propaganda. It would emerge as the central core of Nazi ideology after 1933. There are several phases of racial policy, especially Jewish policy, that one can identify as a way of organizing one's thinking about the regime and the evolution of its policy.

In the first phase from 1933 down to 1935, there was an initial burst of legislation in 1933 we'll talk about. There was an attempt to boycott Jewish businesses, which was called off abruptly; elimination of Jews from civil service jobs, the practice of law and medicine, and so on. But after an initial burst of activity, in early '33, there was nothing really coming from the national regime. There were things called individual actions, *Einzelaktionen* is the German term, local Nazi rowdies, local Nazi fanatics who would harass and humiliate Jews in public, without any sort of authorization from above, but on their own. In 1935, those *Einzelaktionen*, those "individual actions" against Jews, were largely pushed aside, and a more orderly form of anti-Semitism to be introduced by the government. This was a period that would be dominated by a policy of segregation and emigration.

That is, in 1935, the Nazis would introduce a series of laws called the Nuremberg laws, which would in effect make Jews non-citizens of Germany. This was the segregation: Jews losing their civil rights and being treated not as citizens, but subjects of, the Third Reich. And policy in the mid '30s—a period when the SS would emerge for the first time as the real leader in Nazi racial policy—the policy was to encourage Jews to leave. This was not like the Soviet Union after the Second World War; it was difficult for Jews to get out. Official Nazi policy was to encourage them to leave, albeit leaving virtually all of their belongings, all of their property and money, behind. Of course, Jews wishing to leave did not exactly find a welcoming, hospitable world out there willing to take them in.

In 1938, policy would shift again. At the beginning of '38, the Nazis introduced a series of measures to identify Jewish assets in Germany. It was clearly the prelude to some sort of seizure of Jewish assets. The regime was moving, trying to get prepared for some sort of wartime economy. Then in November of 1938 would come, in many ways, the most pivotal and terrifying moment of Nazi racial policy before the war, and that was the so-called "Night of Broken Glass," the *Reichskristallnacht*, in November of 1938, which was the first nationally organized act of violence against Jews—a pogrom, authorized and conducted by the regime itself.

The final phase of Nazi policy would be the war itself. The war would bring, first of all, the Nazis into contact with the largest Jewish populations in Europe, in Poland and in the Soviet Union. Nazi victories over Poland and the Soviet Union—when at least it seemed that the Nazis were winning the war against the Soviets—gave the Nazis an expanding horizon of possibility there, and the Nazis began seeking what they called a "final solution to the Jewish question." That "final solution," of course, would be mass murder. So those are the phases of Nazi racial policy that would be introduced piecemeal.

One of the controversies surrounding racial policy before the war, before one can really talk about the Holocaust, is whether the Nazis were acting according to some sort of game plan. Was there a blueprint for action? Did Hitler enter power already with the idea that he wanted to eliminate the Jews? This was clear; it was there, you can recall, in that first written document we have of Hitler's political life, where he talks about the goal was to eliminate the Jews altogether. What did that mean? What did he think it meant? What did his paladins think it meant? Did it mean mass murder? Did it mean physical extermination? Did it mean forcing Jews to leave Germany? Did it mean setting up a colony for Jews—this was something that was talked about with the so-called Madagascar Plan, that we'll talk about, during the war—or some sort of Jewish reservation far out in the Soviet Union after the Soviet Union had been defeated? Is there a straight line from the pages of *Mein Kampf* to the ovens at Auschwitz?

And that the Nazis may have tacked this way and tacked that way as the circumstances of the exigencies of politics demanded, but that basically, the target was there from the beginning, and it was just a step-by-step implementation. Or is there a more complicated explanation that's required, one that says there's an ideological direction to policy, but it doesn't necessarily mean this particular outcome? There are lots of possible outcomes. When Kruschev pounded his shoe on the table and said to the West, "We will bury you," did he mean that literally? "We're going to destroy you with a massive attack and we'll bury you?" Did he mean over the course of a century that the Socialist system would overcome capitalism, that capitalism was doomed? What did he mean? How does one translate that into policy?

This is a problem for all governments, not just these totalitarian ones or authoritarian ones. How does one take a public opinion poll that shows people are in favor of, let's say, national healthcare and then turn it into an actual policy? Once you start doing that, you see there are all these varieties of possibilities and all these problems that come up. This is exactly what many have argued happens with the National Socialists. They didn't necessarily have a clear idea of what was meant by elimination, and that elimination meaning physical extermination was as much a result of complicated bureaucratic politics within the regime, as it was the ideology itself. There are smart ways to argue either of these positions, and there are not-so-smart ways to argue them, and we will certainly be looking at those. Let's turn our attention to this first phase of racial policy from 1933 to '35.

On April 1, the Nazis introduced a boycott of Jewish shops. It was intended to be open-ended, go on indefinitely. There was crazy reasoning behind it, inverted logic about it, which was that the international Jewish press was spreading atrocity stories about the new Germany, and that therefore one way to show that this wasn't true was to boycott Jewish shops. It was retaliation. It was a disaster from beginning to end. It was unpopular at home; the German population, by all reports from foreign diplomats, reported that it was not popular. It was one thing to listen to the Nazis go on about anti-Semitism, another to see these SA bully boys out in front of a Jewish bakery, with whom your family has traded forever, and seeing them outside, forcing the Jewish proprietor to scrub the sidewalk with a toothbrush. This did not play well, and of course it didn't play well abroad, either. It was called off after 24 hours. They'd overstepped.

There were dismissals in the civil service, in the courts, newspapers. Universities fired people, just assuming that this is what the Nazis wanted them to do, getting ahead of the game, ahead of the curve. All the schools in Germany were state schools, so all the teachers, from kindergarten through the university, were civil servants, so when the Nazis banned Jews from holding civil service positions, that meant all people, all the way down the line. Laws were introduced saying that Jews could not take the bar, could not practice law. Jewish doctors could only treat Jewish patients. These attempts in 1933 to take active steps even brought a response from Hindenburg, who wrote a public letter to Hitler saying, "Surely you don't mean to say that Jewish veterans of the Great War are going to lose their jobs in the civil service, or their ability to practice law?" And the Nazis backtracked and said, "Oh, no, of course not, not veterans," which indicates again, in early '33, the sensitivity that Hitler had to Hindenburg.

A law for the restoration of the professional civil service was passed in April of '33, removing non-Aryans—nobody knew what that meant; there was no working definition of it—and it was finally decided that one Jewish grandparent meant that you were Jewish and therefore you were not Aryan. People were scrambling for family trees, doing genealogy. National Socialist Germany was a boon for genealogists. A law limiting Jewish access to the schools was introduced, a law on revocation of naturalization and annulment of German citizenship was passed; a great many Eastern European Jews had moved into Germany during the Weimar years.

One of the terrible ironies of Nazi racial policy, and then ultimately the terrible ghastly results of it, was that Germany in the period before the First World War and through the 1920s had been seen as a great haven, particularly for Eastern European Jews. Outside the United States, it's the place that Eastern European Jews came, because Jews enjoyed equal rights. Before, it was the most integrated Jewish community in Europe. This law revoked the citizenship of those Polish, Russian, Ukrainian Jews who'd come to Germany, particularly in the 1920s, and those people were then supposed to be returned to Poland, only the Polish government wouldn't accept them back. A hereditary farm law was introduced. No one could inherit a farm unless he could show that he had no Jewish blood going back to 1800. Nobody understood exactly how this would work out. This is why family trees became extremely important.

It's in this context, too, that one has to see the Nuremberg Laws of 1935. After this first burst of legislation that the Nazis passed, the national government seemed to lose interest in the question altogether; mainly, I think, because Hitler and company were concentrating on consolidation of power. As a consequence, they were very happy to let local Nazis run amok, the *Einzelaktionen*, the local harassment of Jews, without the national government having to do much. But by December of 1935, this had gotten quite out of hand. The Nazis were in charge now. The Minister of the Interior Frick said, "We can't all this. Party members are taking the law into their own hands. We can't have it. We have to bring these *Einzelaktionen* under control."

There was another factor too, and that was that Germany had been awarded the Olympic games for 1936. The last thing this government wanted to do was to have hundreds of international journalists descending upon Berlin, traveling around the country, and being treated to these unbelievably ugly sights of the harassment of Jewish shopkeepers and so on. It's in this context, then, that one must view the Nuremberg Laws of 1935. They were announced at the Nuremberg party rally, suddenly and unexpectedly. Hitler had wanted to end the rally with a big speech on foreign policy, but at the last minute changed his mind and said, for policy reasons, he couldn't do it. What he wanted, he said then, was, "What about something on race?"

The bureaucrats in Berlin, who'd been working up some things on this, scrambled around—the first drafts of the Nuremberg laws were written on napkins in a beer hall in Nuremberg—came up with laws which came to be known as the Nuremberg Laws, law for the protection of German blood and German honor. That law forbade marriage between Aryans and Jews. It banned sexual relations between Aryans and Jews, and Jews were not allowed to employ women under 45 in their households. This is basic Racism 101, to attribute to Jews the voracious sexual appetite of Jewish males who were going to devour pure Aryan women. Not only that, the laws were made retroactive, so you can imagine what this meant. Somebody would call up the Gestapo with an anonymous tip: "Frau Braun, back in 1928, had an affair with Herr Goldfarb." Nobody could prove it, but the phone call has been made, so you could see the chicanery that could come of this, people instrumentalizing the laws.

And the Reich citizenship law which was announced, but not promulgated until a bit later, distinguished between a subject and a citizen. Jews were not allowed to be citizens of the Third Reich. There were some problems with the Reich citizenship law, and that is, who is Jewish? The regime couldn't agree. Certain party officials wanted it to be, three Jewish grandparents meant you were Jewish. State officials, all Nazis too, said one Jewish grandparent versus three. The party wanted one; other officials wanted three. Nobody could agree. They went to Hitler; Hitler wouldn't decide. This was quite typical; he said, "I can't be bothered with these sorts of things." His idea was to let them fight it out. And so, for years, this went on, who is Jewish and who is not. There were different gradations: Jewish first, *mischung zuerst grad*, a mixture of the first degree, one Jewish parent. Finally, it was decided that it took three Jewish grandparents to be considered a Jew, or just two Jewish grandparents if one of them was practicing religious. It's both racial, and then this bizarre sort of thing.

In the mid '30s, it would be the SS after the Nuremberg Laws didn't solve the so-called Jewish problem. The SS would now step in and become the major agency dealing with the Jewish issue. Their policy was one called *Entjüdung*. It's a very ugly word in German, and it's just as ugly in English; it means "de-Jewification." Get the Jews out; eliminate the Jews from Germany by encouraging them to leave—to make life unpleasant enough that they would seek a haven elsewhere.

This was SS policy, and the policy that Germany would pursue down to the critical year of 1938, where the party began attempting to identify Jewish assets in order to seize them down the road. And then would come this awful event in November of 1938, the *Reichskristallnacht*.

We'll stop here, because I want to talk about the events of the *Kristallnacht* in November alongside the foreign policy issues, because these events take place—this event in particular—in the aftermath of Hitler's greatest foreign policy triumph. And the two were mixed together in German consciousness, so what might have been seen as the ugliest, the most obvious, miserable act of oppression by the regime comes at a time when Hitler had just achieved his greatest foreign policy victory. We'll take up foreign policy in our next lecture.

Lecture Eight
Hitler's Foreign Policy

Scope:

Thus far, the lectures have focused on essentially domestic affairs after 1933. In this lecture, we will shift our attention to Nazi foreign policy. It will not do to think of Hitler as simply a "madman bent on world domination." Instead, we must focus on Hitler's conception of the international system and Germany's anticipated role in it. Hegemony over the European continent, Hitler believed, was Germany's rightful position, and to achieve this, he would have to demolish the Versailles Treaty and the system it had created. As a result, Hitler's actions between 1933 and 1939 were based on a determination to undo the treaty and position Germany to launch a drive for *Lebensraum* ("living space") in the east. Ultimately, a showdown with the Soviet Union would be necessary, but in the meantime, Hitler was willing to take intermediate steps as the opportunity arose. The implementation of this aggressive policy led Europe and the world rapidly down the slippery slope to global war.

Outline

I. Hitler's conception of international politics.

    A. There was a triangular relationship among Hitler's racial policy, his desire to create "living space" for the German people, and his crusade against "Judeo-Bolshevism" in the East. Ultimately, Hitler wanted to create a greater German Reich that was economically independent.

    B. Hitler envisioned a political division of the world among several leading "empires."

        1. Germany would dominate the European continent.

        2. Britain would continue to have its global empire.

        3. The United States would be the dominant power in the Western hemisphere, but Hitler believed that the U.S. would eventually collapse because of its racial heterogeneity.

        4. Japan would dominate much of Asia.

    C. Germany participated in the Geneva Disarmament Conference of 1933.

1. Hitler agreed to disband all his armed forces—which were quite small anyway—if the other European powers did so as well.
2. When they balked, as Hitler knew they would, he withdrew from the conference and from the League of Nations (to which Germany had been admitted in 1926).
3. There was growing international sentiment, especially in Britain, that the Versailles settlement was, indeed, unjust to Germany. The treaty was universally hated by Germans.

D. Hitler took several steps to re-arm Germany.
1. In 1935, he announced the formation of a German Air Force (*Luftwaffe*). This move was protested ineffectually by the League of Nations.
2. In the Anglo-German Naval Agreement, Germany pledged to keep her fleet to one-third the size of Great Britain's.
3. In 1935, Hitler announced that Germany would institute conscription and build an army.
4. This was followed by the remilitarization of the Rhineland in 1936, in violation of the Treaty of Versailles and other conventions. Although his advisors had counseled against the move, Hitler went ahead with the gamble and was never challenged.
5. Hitler also sent forces to Spain to support Franco in the Spanish Civil War, regarded by many historians as a training ground for Fascist forces that subsequently fought in World War II.

E. Berlin's hosting of the 1936 Olympics seemed to verify Germany's return to great-power status and prestige in the world.

F. In a top-secret conference in November 1937, Hitler laid out to his generals and diplomats what seemed to be a blueprint for his next diplomatic steps to achieve "living space" in the east by 1943–1945. He was certain that war would result.

II. German foreign policy became increasingly aggressive during 1938. Hitler's popularity at home reached its pinnacle.

A. In the spring of 1938, Austria sought international guarantees of sovereignty, but it was eventually annexed by Hitler (the *Anschluss*).

B. Europe was set to begin its slide toward the outbreak of war.

Essential Reading:

Taylor, A. J. P., *The Origins of the Second World War*.

Kershaw, Ian, *Hitler: 1936–1945 Nemesis*.

Supplementary Reading:

Bullock, Alan, *Hitler: A Study in Tyranny*.

Questions to Consider:

1. To what extent was Hitler's foreign policy driven by Nazi ideology? What role did circumstance and improvisation play in the events of 1933–1938?

2. Why was the reaction of the West so tepid in the face of Hitler's aggressive foreign policy? How could Hitler justify his claims to Austria?

Lecture Eight—Transcript
Hitler's Foreign Policy

Hello, and welcome to our eighth lecture on the history of Hitler's empire. We spoke in our last lecture about the evolution of Nazi racial policy from 1933 up to the *Kristallnacht* in November of 1938. I had begun by saying that one of the most difficult things we're asked to do in history is to juggle simultaneity of events, to keep events the way people might have seen them at the time. Now, having traced one of the most controversial features of Nazi domestic policy through the 1930s, I want to turn now to Nazi foreign policy. It was Nazi foreign policy, in particular Hitler's very prominent association with it, that was one of the most popular aspects of the regime.

The Nazis had come to power, of course, with their program of restoring German grandeur, undoing the hated Treaty of Versailles, restoring the German military to a position of prominence, for Germany once again to take its place among the powerful nations of the world. Between 1933 and 1938, Hitler would register a series of extremely impressive foreign policy victories that, in many ways, overcame the reservations that some had about his government and particularly domestic policy. One often hears things about Nazi foreign policy and Hitler's conception of it in particular; this sort of madman's rush for world domination, a boundless adventurism, determination to expand at all costs across Europe and then possibly around the globe. There was a very famous SA song that contributed this. The song went (I'll say it in German first) *"Heute da hort uns Deutschland, und morgen die ganze welt."* That means, "Today Germany is listening to us, and tomorrow the whole world will." But in German, with a very slight change of a prefix , it is *"Heute gehort uns Deutschland, und morgen die ganze welt,"* which means "Today Germany belongs to us, and tomorrow the whole world will."

That was the sense one has of Nazi foreign policy, of Hitler being absolutely maniacal and fanatic in his determination, driven by ideological goals that would drive Germany toward war. But this is not the picture that Hitler presented to the German public, and Hitler operated on the basis of his own notion of the international system. He had a conception of foreign policy. He certainly had basic goals; these were laid out in the 25 Points of the NSDAP in 1920. *Lebensraum* in the east, living space in the east. Germany, Hitler

©2001 The Teaching Company.

argues, is a *volk ohne raum*, a people without space. Traditionally, Germans have looked eastward, in many ways the way Americans looked at the west. It was the Wild West, and for the Germans, the Wild East. The east was there to be colonized, clearly after the First World War, when new states were created.

Poland, a new state—it really wasn't a new state; there had been a Poland, a quite sizable one for centuries, which had then been annexed out of existence in the late 18th century—now is restored as a large Polish state, with a corridor that would attach it to the Baltic Sea and with the port Danzig being under League of Nations administration. But Poland; Czechoslovakia, a completely new creation; Yugoslavia, farther south, all seemed to a great many people not quite legitimate states. The Nazis certainly didn't see them as legitimate. The *Lebensraum*, the living space, was to be gained in the east. Of course, beyond those states lay the real prize, and that was the Soviet Union—the great agricultural potentialities of Russia, Ukraine—and these beckoned to the Nazis in particular.

Hitler wanted to create an autarchic greater German Reich; that is, an economically independent German Reich, one that could withstand, for example, blockades such as England imposed on Germany during the Great War and had led to starvation of tens of thousands and diseases related to dietary problems during the First World War, so an autarchic, an economically independent, German Reich. What that meant was probably going to be the seizure of territory in the east, and there was an ideological element to this as well. This wasn't just a traditional notion of expansion to the east. For Hitler, the great objective was, from the beginning of his career to the end, the showdown with the Soviet Union. Russia wasn't just Russia any longer; it was now the center of Judeo-Bolshevism. So, what might have been a geopolitical objective—seize land, living space, in Russia—now would become also a crusade to rid the world of this terrible Judeo-Bolshevist threat.

These were there from almost the beginning of Hitler's foreign policy discussions, his speeches. He viewed the world; he had a notion of the way the international system should operate. His view of Germany was that Germany's historical and rightful position would be to be the hegemonic power on the continent of Europe—the dominant power on the continent—that Great Britain would have its empire all around the world, which Germany wouldn't threaten;

that there would be a community of interest between Britain and Germany; that Germany would be a bulwark against Bolshevism on the continent of Europe; England's global empire would not be threatened.

Across the Atlantic, there was the United States, which Hitler thought was legitimately the dominant power, and should be the dominant power, in the Western hemisphere. But he also thought, in the long run, that the United States was doomed, that you could not have a country of such racial mixture that could survive over the long haul. But for all intents and purposes, for the foreseeable future, the United States would be the legitimate dominant power in the Western hemisphere. And then beyond, across the Pacific, there was Japan: the Aryans of the East, he sometimes called them. The Japanese would have a legitimate claim to dominate Asia. These would be the four powers that would operate in this world system, this international system, as Hitler envisioned it. What Hitler was really talking about, what he envisioned, was Germany's ability to act much the way a superpower would act. The term didn't exist, superpower, but if it had, it would have been appropriate to Hitler's view, that these would be the four superpowers in a multi-polar world.

All of this meant, in practical terms, not only the revision of the Treaty of Versailles, but its absolute destruction. Publicly, Hitler talked about equality. In all of his public statements from the moment he became chancellor, right down to when the first shots were fired in 1939, it was always about equality. Germany had been denied its rightful position by the Treaty of Versailles, and now all Germany wanted to do was to restore its rightful position, to reclaim it. Other countries had armies. The Czechs had an army, the Poles had an army, the Austrians had an army, but not Germany. So equality, the ability to defend itself, and peace.

Hitler would always say in his speeches, and he would always have these long warm-ups to the speech where he would circle around the main topic, would always be that, "Other world leaders might think about war, but if they suspect me of having warlike intentions, they're all wrong. I'm a veteran of the front; I was there in the trenches, and I know what war means, and I'm not in favor of war, I don't want war. The German people want peace, and that's what I want, but we want peace with equality. There must be equality."

Once these were perfectly reflected in his first foreign policy action, Germany was already a participant in a world disarmament conference, and at that conference, Hitler decided to make a splash.

His representative at the conference, Germany's representative, made a dramatic proposal: Germany would completely disarm if France, Britain, the United States, Japan, Russia—all the other powers—would disarm too. Since Germany only had an armed force of 100,000 troops, this wasn't much of an offer. When the French balked at this—they didn't say "no" immediately, but it was clear they weren't going to do it—Hitler in a huff withdrew Germany's representation from the conference, withdrew from the League of Nations, which was involved in it, and said, "You see? They're not really interested in equality; they're not really interested in justice. This evil system that was set up by the Treaty of Versailles is there to keep Germany down. All we want is the same ability to defend ourselves that every other nation has. Why don't we?"

This played very well at home. First of all, it was thumbing his nose at the Western powers that were responsible for Versailles. It's hard to over-emphasize the degree to which that treaty was unpopular in Germany. It didn't matter if you were the most radical Communist, whether you were a moderate Catholic Center Party member, or whether you were a Nazi. The Versailles Treaty was universally hated as unfair, the reparations that had come with it unfair, everything associated with it unfair. This would then be Hitler's approach, to emphasize Germany's determination to revise the treaty. There was nothing in this that was particularly shocking. All German politicians since 1919 had talked about revising the treaty. Even Gustav Stresemann, whom we mentioned, who had tried to fulfill the treaty between '24 and '28, had done so, so that he could reveal to the Allies how impossible it was to do it, to pay the reparations and so on, how unjust it was. So there was nothing particularly unusual about Hitler's public stance that he wanted to get rid of the treaty, to revise it, to smash it.

In 1935, the Saar, a region in the southwest of Germany which had been put under League of Nations auspices since the end of the war and had been administered by the League, was now given the opportunity to hold a plebiscite. Did it wish to stay in that status, or did it wish to become part of Germany? The vote in the Saar in 1935 was overwhelmingly to come back to Germany, to go *heim ist Reich*, they called it, to return to the Reich, come home to the Reich. This was trumpeted of course by the Nazis as a great success. One of the great principles of the Treaty of Versailles had been the national self-determination of peoples. This had been one of the reasons that Woodrow Wilson believed that Europe had gone to war in 1914—was frustrated, legitimate desire for national unification, or national sentiments. Hence, the creation of Poland, the creation of Czechoslovakia, Yugoslavia, and so on after the war.

The Germans had always felt that the way that that principle had been applied was that if it worked against Germany's interest, fine. Whenever there was a case where national self-determination of peoples would work in Germany's favor, it was blocked by the Allies. In fact, that's not an unreasonable way to view this. In 1919, the Austrians, what was left of rump German Austria, had wished to become united with Germany, only to be blocked by the Allies. The French and the British said, "We fought the Germans for four years and got away by the skin of our teeth. We're not going to have a larger Germany now than we did back in 1914." There were other instances of this, areas along the German-Polish border, for example. So, Hitler's view, and the way he presented this, was always, "We've got legitimate claims on the basis of national self-determination of peoples that were just completely ignored, suppressed by the victors at Versailles."

But the theme that certainly occupied him most was this theme of national defense. Germany is defenseless, surrounded by potential enemies in the center of Europe. It has no way to defend itself. In 1935, March 1, Hitler announced his determination to build an air force, a *Luftwaffe*. This was specifically banned by the Treaty of Versailles. Hitler argued, in typical fashion, that while the British were modernizing their air force, and if Britain was going to modernize its air force to give it more striking power, then Germany needed to be able to defend itself, hence the air force. There was protest from the predictable sources, the French in particular, but no real concerted action against this German decision. So, two weeks later, on March 15, Hitler announced that he was going to introduce conscription. He was going to build a German army that, within a year, would be half a million men in size, and that it would grow after that.

Justification? The others had already shown themselves back in 1933 as being opposed to disarmament. Germany had offered to disarm; they wouldn't do it, so now Germany has to defend itself. Again, protest, but no real concerted action against the German position. In fact, Hitler also announced, just to make explicit what he'd done, he was renouncing the Versailles clauses on re-armament. The League of Nations certainly lodged a protest, but it fell on deaf ears.

Then, in March of 1936, on March 7, Hitler moved German troops into the Rhineland. The West Bank of the Rhine close to Cologne was still part of Germany; it had been part of the Weimar Republic and now was part of the Third Reich. But according to the treaty, that area of the Rhineland was to be demilitarized—no German troops allowed. This was extremely important—small piece of real estate, but strategically important—because as long as there were no German troops in the Rhineland, if the Germans got obstreperous, French troops could simply march across the Franco-German border, be in the Rhineland, and be at the Ruhr, the industrial heartland of Germany, in a flash, just as they'd done in 1923. The decision to remilitarize the Rhineland meant that France was going to be deprived of its one bit of military leverage in dealing with the Germans.

All of Hitler's generals argued against this move. The high command of the army said, "This is crazy. If the French send so much as a battalion of troops into the Rhineland, we can't stop them. It'll be a humiliation on a grand scale." His diplomats advised him not to do it. Hitler overrode their objections and rolled the dice. It wouldn't be the last time. Again, objections, but nothing, no real action. In fact, the British didn't even really protest. This was a worrisome matter to the French, but it shouldn't have been because the British had already made a deal with the Germans, the British saying, "You can rebuild the fleet, as long as it's no larger than one-third the size of the British." For the French, looking at this, they thought, "*Mon Dieu*, the British have sold us out. They're supposed to be enforcing the Treaty of Versailles, and instead, they're cutting their own deal with Hitler."

The French couldn't trust the British, they believed. Nobody could trust the Americans, who were at home with their sidewalks rolled up in a period of extreme isolation. These actions were taken with protest, but with no real concerted effort to stop what the Germans were doing. Part of the reason for this—I think this is extremely important—by the late 1920s, there had been a sea change in the way the West viewed the Treaty of Versailles. Sidney B. Fay, a very famous and distinguished historian at Harvard, had published a two-volume book called *The Origins of the [Great] World War*, in which a Western scholar, for the first time, argued that Germany had not been solely responsible for the outbreak of the war. Not only had it not been solely responsible, it wasn't even mostly responsible for the outbreak of the war.

There was, by the late 1920s, a growing pacifist movement in Britain and a feeling among the educated elites in Britain and also, I believe, in the United States as well, that the Great War had been a great mistake. What, after all, was the great issue at stake in the First World War? What great principle was at stake? And what was worth the loss of millions of lives? Was the death of the Archduke Franz Ferdinand worth all of that? Was Bosnia-Herzegovina worth world war? The general view tended to be no. Even John Maynard Keynes, who'd been part of the British delegation to Versailles in this period, finally said that even the economic demands and the reparations and so on had been too harsh. So there was an international climate that was conducive for Hitler to play this particular song, that Germany had been mistreated. It had been mistreated about disarmament; it had been mistreated about reparations, it had been mistreated about war guilt. It had been mistreated about national self-determination of peoples.

Then in 1936 came the jewel in the crown as far as Nazi foreign policy was concerned, and that was the Olympic games. The world came to Berlin. The country was cleaned up—we talked about racial policy in the last lecture. Part of the reason for the end of the *Einzelaktionen*, these individual acts of harassment by local Nazi radicals against Jews, was to present the best possible view of the new Germany to all the journalists and tourists who would be coming to the games. Americans know one story about the 1936 Olympics and one story only, and that is, of course, Jesse Owens, the great African-American athlete who won gold medal after gold medal, and what a great embarrassment this was to Hitler. Owens certainly did dominate the Olympics in track and field, as the Americans did, as they always had done.

But the Germans won the 1936 Olympics, winning—I always insult people, so if there's anyone listening who is unhappy with this—all these sort of obscure events where you ride and shoot and swim and do a variety of things—shooting, horseback riding, and so on, the Germans dominated and they won. And for Hitler, far from the '36 Olympics being an embarrassment, it was a great public relations victory. Not only that, to remind everyone of exactly what the international environment was like about matters of race, or about anti-Semitism, the American track team, the Olympic coach, pulled a Jewish athlete from the last relay team and replaced him with Jesse Owens; it was a foregone conclusion the Americans were going to win, and so it didn't really make any difference. He pulled the athlete because he didn't want to put Hitler in the embarrassing position of having to receive a Jewish athlete. So it isn't as if somehow Nazi anti-Semitism in this period was sending out shock signals of outrage to the rest of the world. And the world had come to Berlin. And Germany showed off.

In '36, Hitler would also send troops and equipment to help Francisco Franco in Spain fight against the Republic of Spain. Mussolini, in many ways Hitler's model in Italy, had done the same, sending Italian troops. What this did was to position Hitler to draw closer to Mussolini—to find an ally in Europe—and also to help drive the wedge between Mussolini and England and France. Mussolini enjoyed very good publicity and stood in very good standing, in England in particular. The Spanish Civil war would be a problem, and Hitler was quick to take advantage of it.

In 1937, a year when there wouldn't be a dramatic foreign policy victory of the Nazis, there was, however, a meeting, a very famous and very controversial meeting, a secret meeting between Hitler and his foreign policy advisors and his top military people. No notes were to be taken at the meeting, but a colonel, by the name of Hossbach, did take notes, and those notes have become now known as the Hossbach Memorandum. In that memorandum, we read that Hitler had laid out his foreign policy and military goals for the foreseeable future, that Hitler believed that Germany needed and would achieve *Lebensraum* somewhere between 1943 and 1945. This would call for probably the annexation of both Austria and Czechoslovakia. There's no mention of Poland; there's no mention of the Soviet Union.

The military people present, two generals, both complained—this was still a time when this was possible—and in a very congenial fashion, that this looked like a tall order for the German army to do, and that surely this would involve them in a war in the West with England and France, and did Germany really want to fight a two-front war? Then the foreign minister, Baron von Neurath, also raised concerns that this would lead to a two-front war, and so on. What's controversial about the memorandum is what it means.

Was Hitler sort of giving a tour of the rise and talking in very general terms that he wanted by 1943–45 Germany to be prepared for a showdown—a war—for *Lebensraum*? Or was this a kind of timetable? He mentions Austria and Czechoslovakia. Was he thinking in very concrete terms, "This will be my next step. This will be the next step in order to achieve these goals?" It's been interpreted in both ways: as a blueprint, or a typical kind of Hitler oration, in which he's talking in very general terms. We know certainly that, within a year, the two military leaders, generals Fritz and Blomberg, were both removed from their positions in the German army, and Baron von Neurath, the foreign minister, was also replaced by a Nazi named Joachim von Ribbentrop as foreign minister. So these potential obstacles on the road to Hitler's policy had been removed.

What would follow in 1938 would be the high point of Hitler's foreign policy achievements for the war, and also the pinnacle of Hitler's popularity at home. In early 1938, Austria became very nervous about German designs. There was a German Nazi Party in Austria; it had been banned in 1934, but they were still there. There were still lots of protests, a lot of Nazis in Austrian prisons, but also a lot who were demanding some sort of *Anschluss*, some sort of linkage with Germany, which the Austrian government certainly did not want. The Prime Minister of Austria, named Kurt von Schuschnigg, sought support from Italy, from France, from England, took soundings to see if there was any guarantee of Austrian sovereignty. He didn't receive any, but the Germans found out about it, and provoked a crisis.

The Nazis argued that this action showed lack of faith by the Austrians; there'd been an agreement between Austria and Germany in 1934, in which Germany and Austria tried to talk about coordinating their policies. At the last moment, when it looked like

Hitler might, in fact, be willing to actually invade Austria over this, the German ambassador to Vienna, an old friend by the name of Franz von Papen (who had more lives than a cat) resurfaced. He was supposed to have been killed in the Night of Long Knives, when Gregor Strasser and Ernst Rohm had been killed in '34, but hadn't been home. He'd gotten away, and now surfaced as ambassador. He suggested a bit of summit diplomacy, and that summit diplomacy was to lead to Schuschnigg to Berchtesgaden, to meet Hitler at Hitler's home there.

Schuschnigg traveled to Salzburg, went across the border, was taken in motorcade up to Hitler's place in Berchtesgaden, but not at the usual big house, but went round and round and round a mountain in a long motorcade of cars, got out in a parking lot, and it looked like just the side of a mountain there, when he realized that there was an opening in a tunnel. Two enormous doors opened, and Schuschnigg was led inside, all the way down this long tunnel with torch lights all the way down, where SS men in dress uniform, white gloves, helmets, bayonets—they walked down the long hall into a room, a small room, which Schuschnigg realized was actually moving. It was an elevator. He was taken to the top of the mountain, the elevator doors opened, and there was Hitler with the high command of the German army.

Hitler gave an ultimatum that Schuschnigg should give in, allow certain things, free the Nazis, and so on, which Schuschnigg refused to do. He somehow got off the mountain in one piece, went back to Vienna, and said, "We'll have a plebiscite in four days to determine this." This sent Hitler into a fury. There was going to be no plebiscite, and so the Nazis, in effect, forced an ultimatum on Schuschnigg. The Austrian government caved in, and there was an *Anschluss*, a linkage between Germany and Austria. Hitler moved into Austria with great cheering crowds on his way to Vienna and announced to everybody's surprise—nobody had really thought he was going to annex Austria—that Austria had now become a part of Germany. He had fulfilled his childhood dream, he said, of bringing the Germans of Austria and Germany together in one *Gross Deutsche Reich*, one greater German Reich.

As soon as that was done, Czechoslovakia moved from the back burner to the front, and Europe was set to begin a slide toward the outbreak of war in 1939, as events in 1938 came to a close. It was in this situation, however, that the *Reichskristallnacht*—this great pogrom against the Jews of Germany occurred in November—has to be placed in public awareness against this great foreign policy victory and the other which would come in October, the seizure of the Sudetenland in the Munich conference.

Lecture Nine
Munich and the Triumph of National Socialism

Scope:

By the provisions of the Munich Pact of 1938, the Sudetenland was ceded to Germany. The German invasion of Czechoslovakia soon followed. In August 1939, Nazi Germany and the Soviet Union signed a cynical non-aggression pact that allowed Hitler to invade Poland, sealing the fate of Poland and peace in Europe. On September 1, 1939, Hitler sent his troops into Poland, triggering a European-wide war.

Outline

I. A crisis over the Sudetenland in Czechoslovakia developed in late summer; German nationals in the area claimed harassment by the Czech government and appealed to Berlin. Prague mobilized its troops, and Europe appeared on the verge of war.

   A. Mussolini intervened in support of Hitler's territorial claim, and Neville Chamberlain sought to negotiate a solution.

   B. Chamberlain was pursuing a policy of "appeasement."

   C. In September 1938, by terms of the Munich Pact, England, France, Germany, and Italy agreed to cede the Sudetenland to Germany. Russia was not invited to the Munich Conference.

   1. There was some opposition to this move in the German army. Chief of Staff Ludwig Beck resigned in protest of Hitler's apparent determination to go to war over the Sudetenland. The opposition in the army was dashed by the West's capitulation at Munich.

   2. In March 1939, Germany invaded Czechoslovakia, violating the Munich Pact. The Czechs did not resist. England, backed by France, issued a guarantee of Polish territory and sovereignty, because another crisis seemed to be brewing over German claims in Poland.

II. The final crisis.

   A. In the late summer of 1939, the key to the diplomatic situation was in Moscow.

1. Soviet leader Josef Stalin realized (more clearly than ever after Munich) that the West was weak. He feared that the Western powers sought to divert German aggression toward the East.
2. Nazi foreign minister Joachim Ribbentrop and his Soviet counterpart V.M. Molotov signed a non-aggression pact in late August 1939 that provided for the German and Russian partition of Poland.
3. Although the two regimes were ideological enemies, both had practical reasons for signing the agreement, which was the death knell for Poland and for peace.

B. On September 1, 1939, Germany launched a *Blitzkrieg* attack on Poland and quickly overwhelmed it from the west.

1. In compliance with their treaty obligations (and contrary to Hitler's expectations), Britain and France declared war on Germany.
2. The European-wide war had begun.
3. The Soviet Union attacked Poland from the east, pursuant to Stalin's non-aggression pact with Germany.

Essential Reading:

Keegan, John, *The Second World War*.

Kershaw, Ian, *Hitler: 1936–1945 Nemesis*.

Supplementary Reading:

Lukacs, John, *The Duel* and *Five Days in London, May 1940*.

Questions to Consider:

1. What were the ideas behind the British policy of appeasement? In retrospect, it seems almost criminally shortsighted, but what constraints did Britain operate under in 1938-1939?
2. What were the implications of the Molotov-Ribbentrop Pact, both within Germany and in the international community? Why did Hitler enter such an agreement with his most hated ideological enemy?

Lecture Nine—Transcript
Munich and the Triumph of National Socialism

Hello. This is our ninth lecture in our series on this history of Hitler's empire. In the eighth lecture, we talked about the diplomatic policy of the National Socialists between 1933 and 1938, and concluded with what, to that point, had been Hitler's greatest achievement in foreign policy. That was his so-called *Anschluss* with Austria in the spring of 1938, his bringing this German Austria into a greater German Reich. Hitler himself saw this as the culmination of a lifelong dream. He'd been born, as we mentioned much earlier, in Braunau Am Inn on the border between Austria and Germany. He had talked in *Mein Kampf* about the bringing together of all Germans into some sort of *Gross Deutsche Reich*, a greater German Reich, and this seemed to be a fulfillment, in part, of that dream and that political objective.

Inside Germany, it was tremendously popular. Hitler had forced the national self-determination of peoples, which had been one of the hallmarks of the Treaty of Versailles, onto the international community. There was great unease in Paris in particular and London and so on about the *Anschluss* with Austria, but, after all, it was national self-determination of peoples. They couldn't argue with it from some sort of principled view. And the Austrians seemed to want this unification. Great scenes of jubilation in Vienna as Hitler spoke in the center of the city; a triumphant procession of Hitler's caravan all the way down from the German border into Vienna. But of course, this is the pubic reaction. Himmler and the SS moved into Austria at the same time, and within two weeks, had arrested 70,000 politically unreliable Austrians.

There would be a plebiscite, but only after the Nazis had established full control in Vienna. No one knows what the outcome of that plebiscite would have been. This was a Catholic country; there were still objections and concerns, especially at this time, by the Vatican about National Socialist Germany. The Vatican had issued an encyclical called *Mit Brennender Sorge*, "With Burning Care," about breaches of the concordant that the Nazis had signed with the Vatican in 1933. And yet, there seemed to be considerable public support. Very few people were able to do what—if you've seen *The Sound of Music*—the von Trapp family apparently did, which is to sing their way across the Alps, from Austria into Switzerland.

That great triumph was just the beginning for National Socialist policy. During the *Anschluss*, Hitler and Goering had worried about the possible reaction of Czechoslovakia to German actions in Austria; they were afraid particularly of military mobilization. The Czech army was sizable, it was very well trained, it was very well armed. So the concern about what the Czechs might do over a German incursion into Austria was considerable. There had been a National Socialist Party in Czechoslovakia, where there was a sizable German population, particularly around the rim of Czechoslovakia that extends into Germany proper, an area called the Sudetenland, a mountain region right on the frontier. The NSDAP in Czechoslovakia, therefore, had been banned. A Sudeten German homefront, headed by a man called Conrad Heinlein, had been established. It was a quasi-Nazi organization of ethnic Germans living in the Sudetenland.

The Sudeten German Party was pro-Nazi; certainly by 1936, it was obvious. And their stated goal was the cession of the Sudetenland from Czechoslovakia. After the *Anschluss* with Austria, Czechoslovakia moved to the forefront of Nazi attention. So great was the concern in Prague, the Czech capital, about the *Anschluss*, that Hitler felt it necessary to send a reassuring telegram to the Czech president, Benes, reassuring him that Germany had no territorial desires in Czechoslovakia, while at the same time, he gave his military men orders to "smash Czechoslovakia in the foreseeable future." Indeed, the date was set for October 1, 1938.

The Sudeten Germans were encouraged by Berlin to make impossible demands, to provoke incidents, whereby the Czech authorities would be seen to oppress the German minority in Czechoslovakia, and in the Sudetenland in particular. In fact, things became so tense that in May of '38, the Czechs had actually, even beforehand, had sensed that they wanted to mobilize their troops, so the concern was there in the summer of 1938, and a diplomatic struggle would ensue. It was clear that the Nazis were pressing, and the Czech government didn't see this as national self-determination of peoples, and the Czech authorities had the ability to resist. So, what would happen if the Germans moved into the Sudetenland or claimed it? Czechoslovakia had treaties with two major European states, one with France and one with the Soviet Union. If Germany moved into the Sudetenland and the Czechs resisted, it would be the tripwire that would start a second European-wide war.

The agreement between France, Russia, and Czechoslovakia was that Russia would come to Czechoslovakia's aid if France did first. Stalin didn't trust the West, and he didn't want to be provoked into a war against Germany. He always thought that basically the West was trying to encourage German expansion to the east at his expense, so for Stalin, the treaty made sense. If France honored its obligation to Czechoslovakia, so too would the Soviet Union. But for diplomats in Europe—and all over the world in fact—concern grew over the summer of 1938 that something would lead to a German invasion, and then this would be the start of a second world war.

It was in these circumstances that Neville Chamberlain decided to intervene at the Nuremberg rally in early September. Hitler called for the Sudetenland to come *heim ist Reich*, to come home to the Reich. There was a long tirade against the Czech oppression of the German minority there. It looked as if he was working himself up into some sort of declaration of war. Neville Chamberlain, the British prime minister, at this point, decided to engage in what we would call summit diplomacy. He would fly to Germany to meet with Hitler. He was not going to be guilty of the same things that his predecessors during this crisis of 1914 had done; that is, simply stand by and let the situation move inexorably toward war. He was going to go. He would show his good will by going to talk to Hitler man to man and see if something could not be worked out.

Chamberlain would visit Hitler in Berchtesgaden in September of 1938, on September 15. What he found was the agreeable Hitler, the charming Hitler, the Hitler who welcomed him. He did the same routine as poor Schuschnigg had done earlier in the year—that is, was taken up to this house up on top of the Eagle's Nest, taken up in the elevator. But when the doors opened for Chamberlain, there was not the general staff of the German army; there was Hitler, bowing, charming. "We want to work this out; we have no designs, we have no desire for war," and so on. But he was very firm about one thing, and that was the German minority in Czechoslovakia was being badly treated, and something had to be done.

Chamberlain left Berchtesgaden, determined to go back to London. He told Hitler he would go back and see if he could win the agreement of the British cabinet to work out some deal about the Sudetenland, probably with a plebiscite involved, where there would be a vote to see whether the Sudetenland really wanted to become part of Germany or remain in Czechoslovakia. He would also use his good offices to convince the French to play ball on this. No mention of the Russians. He went back to London; he did just that, the British cabinet went along. Edouard Daladier, the prime minister of France, was a little more cautious, a little more concerned, but ultimately the French government went along as well. Chamberlain returned to Germany for a second meeting with Hitler, this time at Bad Godesberg on the Rhine.

This time he was full of himself for having pulled off this real coup. He'd convinced the cabinet, he'd convinced the French, he'd found a solution whereby there would be some arrangement where the Sudetenland would have a chance to express its views and would ultimately probably become part of Germany. But this time, he didn't fund the charming Hitler, he found the brash, demanding, fanatical Hitler, who said that the German who simply told him this wasn't good enough, the German people's patience was finished, that the Czechs were persecuting Germans in the Sudetenland—atrocities every day—and that although he was doing his best, he simply couldn't hold back the wrath of the German people toward these atrocities committed against the German minority. Chamberlain left crestfallen, not knowing what to do.

At a speech at the Sportspalast in Berlin shortly thereafter, Hitler demanded agreement on the terms he had put forward—basically immediate German entry into Czechoslovakia. He demanded agreement within 48 hours. It was an ultimatum. At this point, Britain and France actually mobilized their troops. France was going to honor its obligation; the British looked like they were going to do it as well. One way or the other, Hitler threatened, this matter will be resolved by October 1, so it seemed as if a real deadline had been given. The Czechs rejected Hitler's demands, and Europe stood perched on the precipice.

The situation was saved by Benito Mussolini, who, despite the fact that he had made an agreement with Hitler, the Pact of Steel—and Mussolini loved rattling his saber and pounding his chest and talking about the warlike qualities of Italy, and so on—Italy wasn't prepared to go to war, and it certainly was not going to go to war with England and France over a strip of territory in Czechoslovakia that most Italians could not have found with a magnifying glass. Mussolini suggested that he would use his good offices, bring about a conference to settle this crisis, and Chamberlain agreed. So, on September 29, 1938, Chamberlain, Edouard Daladier of France, Mussolini, and Hitler met in the Führerbau, the Führer's offices in Munich, for a conference that has lived in infamy ever since. It was the Munich Conference. If you want to discredit anybody in political life, to this day, all you have to do is say, "It's another Munich, it's appeasement," so great was the criminal myopia of Chamberlain at this point.

The Nazis got what they wanted. German troops moved immediately into Czechoslovakia; the Sudetenland became part of Germany. There was no fighting. Absent at the Munich Conference were the Czechs, whose delegation literally had to stand outside the building, waiting to hear the fate of their country, the news brought to them with great embarrassment by Britain and France. The other party not invited to the conference was the Soviet Union, who still was saying all the way through this that it would honor its obligations to Czechoslovakia.

There's a photograph of this conference after the pact had been signed; the agreement had been signed. I rarely think a picture's worth a thousand words, but this may be one of those cases where it is. There's a picture that shows Chamberlain, who just looks pleased as punch with himself—he's so satisfied; he's saved Europe. He'd saved Europe from war. Over what? This little strip of territory that was, everybody agreed, pretty much ethnically German. Was Europe ready to go to war over that? Millions of people die over this strip of largely German territory that had been ceded to this new Czech State? He thought not, and most people in Europe agreed. Next to him is Edouard Daladier. Daladier has a look on his face like someone who's just supped with the Devil. He knew no good would come of this, and you can read it in his face. Relief is there on the countenance of Mussolini.

And then there's Hitler standing at the end, beaming like the cat who swallowed the canary. He'd gotten exactly what he wanted, and without war. His popularity in Germany soared after this—a great victory. Not only had Germany brought more Germans into this *Gross Deutsche Reich*; Britain and France and Italy had all come to Germany. Germany, under Hitler, had forged its own fate. And of course, back in England, Chamberlain would return and wave the agreement—not the actual Munich agreement, but another agreement made at the time—held it up with those most famous of all famous last words: "I believe this means peace in our time."

The implications of Munich were profound indeed. For one thing, there had been an opposition forming within the German army under General Ludwig Beck. When Hitler gave the orders to prepare an invasion of Czechoslovakia, Beck, who was chief of staff of the army, looked at it and said, "This is suicide. This will not work. The region that Germany would have to invade is all mountains." The Czechs were well armed; they were well trained. They had a large army. Beck thought, "If we invade, we'll be annihilated. The Russians will come in, the French will come in." He began to organize resistance. He resigned his post in protest, and continued to try to convince other high military leaders of the folly of this action. Beck and the military conspirators, who had begun to think it may be time to remove Hitler, were shocked that the West would go along with this. Just as in 1936, when Hitler had moved into the Rhineland over military objections, now Hitler had gambled again, and he'd been proven right and the army wrong.

It also drove the Soviet Union away from the West. It convinced Stalin, who didn't need much convincing at this point, of Western weakness. France and England—anti-Communist states, he believed, particularly England—weren't interested in really holding back the Nazis, only in channeling Nazi aggression to the east. The West could not be relied upon in the crunch, he believed. Hitler, by the way, was convinced of exactly the same thing. The West was weak, vacillating; it wouldn't stand up to its treaty obligations. Later, Hitler would say, as he planned his invasion of Poland and didn't believe the West would intervene, "They won't intervene. I've seen them at Munich. They're worms."

Three weeks later, military plans were already under way for the invasion of what was left of Czechoslovakia. In other words, Hitler wasn't going to be satisfied with just the Sudetenland. In March of 1939, Germany invaded the rump state of Czechoslovakia. Up until this point, all of Hitler's foreign policy moves—remilitarization of the Rhineland, the German territory, the *Anschluss* with Austria (after all, these were Austrians who appeared to want to become part of Germany), the Sudetenland with its largely ethnic German population—all could be justified under the principle of the national self-determination of peoples. He wasn't foolish enough to let anybody have a plebiscite to vote on it, but this is what he could argue.

But in March of 1939, German troops moved across the frontier. The Czech government was in an impossible position. There was no real resistance. The French didn't begin to think about honoring their obligations to Czechoslovakia and neither did the Russians, and the Czech state was absorbed. But so great was the shock of that invasion—it was a naked aggression that Germany had committed— and it forced the hand of the British and French governments. England now issued a pledge to the Polish State, which might logically be the next on Hitler's menu, a guarantee of Polish sovereignty. The French did as well. The question was, would they, in fact, honor any obligations to the Poles? Why would they? Why should they? They hadn't done it all through the '30s, and they had certainly not done it with poor Czechoslovakia.

Hitler began making military plans for an invasion of Poland. There was a strip of territory, the Polish Corridor, that had given the new Polish state after 1919 access to the Baltic Sea. The city of Danzig was administered as a free city by the League of Nations. It was a German city—had been for some time—and so once again, one saw the usual drumroll: German minorities mistreated by the Polish government, some sort of representation for the German minority had to be made, the German population wasn't going to stand for more of this. At this point, so grave was the threat—the sense that war might be imminent—that Franklin Roosevelt took the extraordinary step of writing a public letter to Hitler, in which there was a laundry list of states that he wanted Hitler to say that Germany wasn't going to attack.

And Hitler got up in the Reichstag, now obviously all Nazi, and gave one of his most ironic and sarcastic speeches, in which he goes down all through the list of states and says, "I realize that President Roosevelt, being a great man and leader of a large nation, feels it incumbent on him to speak for the rest of the world, but I, as the chancellor of Germany, in a more humble position, can only speak for my own country. It's not clear that President Roosevelt has actually sounded out all these countries. He couldn't very well talk to the populations of Palestine or Syria, since they're occupied by the British and the French, who wouldn't let them express their views anyway. And if Germany expressed interest or asked similar questions to countries in Latin America, that they would be told by the United States—this is referred to the Monroe Doctrine—and told to mind Germany's own business."

Still, in that speech, Hitler made no promises, and he continued to assert that Danzig wasn't worth a war, he didn't want war; he wanted some solution to this now new Polish problem. Nonetheless, he also gave orders to his military that "Danzig is not the object of our activities. It is a question of expanding our *Lebensraum*, our living space in the east, our food supplies, of settling the Baltic problem. There is no question of sparing Poland, and we are left with the decision to attack Poland at the earliest possible opportunity." So, while publicly protesting that he's trying to find a way for peace, Poland now becomes first on the agenda, and the military is already making plans for an invasion.

Pressure was mounting on Chamberlain's government. Would it indeed honor its obligation to Poland? The key to the diplomatic situation in the summer and early fall of 1939, however, wasn't in London; the key was in Moscow. What would the Soviets do? The British and French had tried at various points over the summer to send out diplomatic feelers to the Soviets, saying, "We're really going to honor our obligations to Poland. The Germans, if they're interested in Poland today, it'll be the Soviet Union tomorrow, and we're really ready to stand firm on this," and so on. But they were low-level contacts; Chamberlain certainly didn't fly off to Moscow to talk with Stalin. Meanwhile, the Germans took this up at a much higher level.

German Foreign Minister Joachim von Ribbentrop had begun to send feelers to his counterpart in the Soviet Union, Molotov, about the possibility of some sort of deal between the Soviet Union and Nazi Germany. Finally, Ribbentrop offered the possibility of a non-aggression pact with the Soviet Union. For Hitler, this pact made no ideological sense whatsoever. These were the two great ideological enemies. If Hitler was determined to smash Judeo-Bolshevism in the Soviet Union, Stalin saw Nazi Germany as the incarnation of evil. It was the great fascist power that was the greatest threat to Socialism, to Communism, in the world. But in a practical sense, there was a good deal of compelling evidence to support signing such a pact.

For one thing, Hitler, who was determined by this point to go to war with Poland—he was going to have his war; as he said, "I'm not going to be cheated out of it like I was in Munch"—he was going to go to war with Poland. He believed that a non-aggression pact with the Soviet Union would act as a deterrent to the West. England and France wouldn't dare intervene if the Soviet Union were already in the same boat as Nazi Germany. What could they do? There was no way they could save Poland, so why would they intervene? It was a deterrent to Western intervention. And of course at the same time and more obviously, it would remove the danger of a two-front war for Germany. This, Hitler always argued, had been Germany's great problem. In the First War, it had fought the Russians in the east and the Western powers on the western front. He was determined to avoid this at all costs, so this deal with the Soviets allowed him to do that. But I think the main thing was that he really didn't believe the West would fight. The West didn't want to fight, and this would be the sealing blow; it would act as a deterrent.

For Stalin, the pact also made sense. Number one, it would buy time. In 1938, the Soviet Union and Stalin had initiated a massive purge of the Red Army. Not just the leadership, not just the generals—the general staff—a purge that went all the way down to company level, inserting political commissars to make sure the army was under direct Bolshevist/Communist control. International intelligence experts believed that the Soviet military was extremely weak as a result—it certainly seemed to be—and so it would buy time to rebuild his military. It would also provide territorial and strategic advantages in Eastern Europe. Any agreement would mean a Soviet move west into part of Poland.

On August 24, Germany and Russia astonished the world by signing a non-aggression pact—the Molotov-Ribbentrop Pact, it was called, or the Nazi-Soviet non-aggression Pact—in Moscow, pledging not to go to war with one another. But also, there were secret clauses, very important secret clauses, really dividing Eastern Europe into spheres of influence. Germany was to get Lithuania and Vilne; the Soviet Union Finland, Estonia, Latvia—these were to be in its sphere of influence. They agreed on a partition of Poland. Germans would move in from the west, the Soviets from the east. They couldn't agree about Romania, which had rich oil fields, but the Molotov-Ribbentrop Pact on August 24, 1939 was the death knell for the state of Poland—and for peace in Europe.

Germany was not prepared for a major war. Despite a four-year plan begun in 1936 to build the German economy, to make it autarchic, economically self-sufficient, it wasn't ready for a long war. It could fight a limited war, such as one against Poland—a diplomatically isolated Poland—but certainly not a long war. It reflected Hitler's conviction that the West wouldn't fight. He could fight a limited war in the east. On September 1, 1939, the German population was awakened to a news bulletin that the Poles had attacked a German radio station on the frontier, and that German troops had been responding. In fact, the Germans had launched a massive invasion of Poland that, within a month, would bring the defeat of the Polish military.

To Hitler's great astonishment, Britain and France decided to honor their obligations. Chamberlain issued an ultimatum to Germany: move out of Poland and then we can talk about the corridor, we can talk about Danzig, we can talk about anything—but not as long as German troops are there. Hitler refused. So astonished was Hitler that the West and then Chamberlain declared war on Germany, as did France—Hitler was so astonished by this that when he heard the news that they had actually declared war, he turned to Ribbentrop, who had guaranteed him they wouldn't, and said to Ribbentrop, "What now?" Germany had made no preparations, as I said, for a long war. They had followed a policy of armaments in breadth, not in depth, so that they had lots of different sorts of military equipment, but it hadn't been built in any sort of depth to sustain a long war.

The Polish campaign was over in a month. The Poles fought heroically against overwhelming German force—you've probably seen photographs or films of Polish cavalry riding out on horseback to do battle against German tanks. Warsaw was bombed, signaling already that this wouldn't be a war like the First War, where there was a distinction between front and the homefront. Now civilians were already on the front line with the bombing of Warsaw. What Hitler had believed would be a short engagement against Poland now threatened to be the European-wide war which he did not believe would happen and was not prepared to fight.

Lecture Ten
War in the West, War in the East

Scope:

In this lecture, we will turn our attention to Hitler's war on the western and eastern fronts. First, we examine the rapid German successes in the west that were halted by the Battle of Britain. We then examine the Nazi ideological view of the Soviet Union as the center of what Hitler invariably referred to as "Judeo-Bolshevism." It was, he believed, Germany's historic duty to smash this world conspiracy and save Western civilization from both Communism and the "pernicious" influence of the Jews. The war in the east, therefore, would be not only a campaign to gain territory (*Lebensraum*, or "living space") for the German nation but a great ideological crusade. It was to be a brutal, no-holds-barred assault, and German troops were issued orders explaining that the usual code of military conduct, the usual rules of war, would not apply in the east. Although England had not broken, Hitler nevertheless launched his attack on the Soviet Union (Operation Barbarossa) in June 1941, believing that the Red Army was severely weakened by Stalin's purges of 1938 and would collapse within weeks.

Outline

I. Would there now be war in the west?

   A. Between the fall of Poland and the spring of 1940, no significant fighting took place in the west.

      1. The English called this period "the Phoney War"; the French, the "*drole de guerre*"; and the Germans, the "*Sitzkrieg.*"

      2. In April 1940, Germany invaded Norway and Denmark.

      3. In May 1940, German units attacked France, Belgium, and Holland and rapidly rolled back the French army, thought to be secure behind the Maginot Line, and drove the British back across the Channel at Dunkirk.

      4. The surprisingly easy victory over France marked the high water mark of Hitler's popularity at home.

   B. In July 1940, Germany began planning an invasion of Britain (Operation Sea Lion) and launched an air assault (the Battle of Britain) against England.

1. Standing alone, the British defeated the German *Luftwaffe* in a series of air battles.
2. Hitler grew impatient—he had not intended a war against Britain—and finally postponed Operation Sea Lion.
3. Still, National Socialist Germany was the master of Europe.

II. The main event: the showdown with the Soviet Union.
   A. Hitler had always believed that war with the Soviet Union was inevitable.
      1. Nazi ideology held the Soviet Union to be the center of a global Judeo-Bolshevist conspiracy.
      2. Thus, war against the Soviet Union would have not only geopolitical objectives, providing the German nation with living space (*Lebensraum*) in the east, but a major ideological goal as well: the destruction of Judeo-Bolshevism.
   B. Hitler also was convinced that the Red Army was weak.
      1. The purges of the Red Army in 1938 had devastated the command structure.
      2. The Soviets had invaded Finland in late 1939, and although the Red Army prevailed, the Finns had put up a tenacious defense. The international intelligence community's evaluation of the Red Army was that it was large and cumbersome.
      3. Hitler believed that the Soviet Union was rotten to the core and would collapse within a matter of weeks.

III. In late spring 1940, Hitler shifted his attention to the east and, despite his non-aggression pact with Stalin, ordered his high command to begin planning for an invasion of the Soviet Union.
   A. Hitler warned his generals that this was to be an ideological war to the finish and German soldiers could not be expected to fight according to the usual rules of war.
      1. Troops were issued the infamous "Commissar Order," instructing them to eliminate all "political commissars [of the Bolshevik party], guerrillas, partisans, and Jews."
      2. Special SS commando units, the *Einsatzgruppen*, would accompany the troops into the Soviet Union and would be given "special tasks."

B. On June 22, 1941, Hitler launched Operation Barbarossa, the largest military undertaking in human history.

    1. In the opening weeks of the invasion, Germany's initial success against the unprepared Russian forces was astounding.

    2. The Germans drove deep into the Soviet Union in a matter of days.

    3. They pushed toward Leningrad in the north, Moscow in the center, and Kiev in the south.

    4. The Soviets suffered staggering casualties.

    5. Virtually the entire Soviet air force was destroyed in just two days.

C. By late summer, however, the German advance slowed; the German military was running low on supplies and had also suffered growing casualties.

    1. Germany had intended to invade before June, but bad weather and Mussolini's ill-advised invasion of Greece forced Hitler to postpone the attack; now Germany paid the price for that delay.

    2. Fall rains slowed the German advance, and in late November and early December, the snows came to Russia's aid.

    3. On December 5–6, the Russians launched a major counteroffensive before Moscow, almost breaking through German lines.

    4. The counteroffensive halted the German advance, and the *Blitzkrieg* phase of the war was over, as were Hitler's hopes for a short war.

    5. On December 7, 1941, the Japanese attacked Pearl Harbor, and four days later, Hitler declared war on the United States; the European war had become the Second World War.

Essential Reading:

Keegan, John, *The Second World War*.

Burleigh, Michael, *The Third Reich*.

Supplementary Reading:

Overy, Richard, *Russia's War*.

Questions to Consider:

1. How were the Germans able to prevail in the west in 1940? How, in particular, does one account for the totally unexpected collapse of France?

2. How and why was the war in the east fought on such different terms as the war in the west?

3. Why did Hitler and his generals believe that they could defeat the Soviet Union in a month to six weeks?

4. Why did Operation Barbarossa fail?

Lecture Ten—Transcript
War in the West, War in the East

Hello, and welcome to this tenth in our series of lectures on the history of Hitler's empire. In our last lecture, we discussed the outbreak—the coming—of the war in Europe, the misassumptions by Hitler about possible British and French responses to a German invasion of Poland. We saw that, within a month, the Polish State, despite heroic efforts on the part of the Polish military and population to resist the Germans, had fallen by October 2. The city of Warsaw had been pounded from the air—a first—setting a new tone, sending a signal that this was to be a different sort of war than the First War. Now the question facing Germany, which had not prepared for a long war, was the responses of England and France. They had surprised Hitler by declaring war, honoring their obligations to Poland, and now the question was, having seen Poland fall, what would the British and French actually do?

Hitler had used a new strategy in the attack on Poland. It was called *Blitzkrieg*, lightning war, the mounting of armored units supported by air power to break through enemy lines and circle the soldiers trapped there in great armored pincers, with an emphasis on speed. The new strategy was a way of overcoming the trench warfare that had bedeviled the militaries of the First World War. The Germans had developed this *Blitzkrieg* strategy as a military strategy, but it also had political implications and economic ones as well. This suited Hitler very nicely. Hitler did not want a long war. He wanted business as usual on the homefront.

One of the things that he was determined to avoid was privation of the German civilian population. He believed, having watched the revolution at the end of 1918 that brought down the old empire, that it was because of this privation at the homefront that the German people had abandoned the Kaiser and that Germany had lost. So a *Blitzkrieg* strategy would mean that you would try to do business as usual. You wouldn't mobilize the economy on a full wartime footing. You would fight a quick, lightning war against a diplomatically and a militarily isolated opponent, which would be settled in a matter of weeks, possibly a month, two months at the most, and then it would be possible to continue day-to-day life inside of Germany. As a consequence, as I indicated in the last lecture, what Hitler had pursued was a policy of armaments in breadth, and not in depth. Germany simply was not prepared for a long war, not for a war against England and France that might drag out, as everyone feared, like the First had done.

What came then, after the fall of Poland, was a very curious period, a period in which, technically, Germany was at war with England and France, but in which nobody was shooting at anybody else. The English and the Americans called it the period of "the Phony War," the French called it the *drole de guerre*, the strange war; the Germans called it the *Sitzkrieg*, the sitting war, as opposed to the *Blitzkrieg*. During this period, there were lots of diplomatic feelers that were sent back and forth, Hitler basically trying to convince the British, "Look. We have no quarrel with you. We don't want to see a war between Great Britain and Germany. Surely you can understand this, and some sort of accommodation can be made." The British response was consistent. It was, "Remove your troops from Poland, and then it will be possible for us to sit down and talk," which the Germans, of course, were unwilling to do. So, through the fall and winter of 1939 and into the spring of 1940, this strange war, this Phony War, this *Sitzkrieg*, prevailed, but it became increasingly clear, with the failure of any sort of diplomatic initiative, that war was coming in the West, and indeed, it did.

In April, German troops attacked into Norway and Denmark to cut off any northern approaches by the British and French to secure a northern front. Then, in May of 1940, German troops struck in the West. Using the same *Blitzkrieg* tactics that had proven so successful against the Poles, the Germans smashed into Holland and Belgium. British and French troops rushed to meet them, and then a major German armored column burst out of the Arden Forest, cutting off the British and French troops in Belgium, swung around, and inflicted a devastating defeat on the French army and on the British.

The British were cut off—between May 28 and June 4, there was this tremendous evacuation of British troops off the beaches at Dunkirk, which was, in many ways, a military miracle; they'd gotten about 300,000 troops off the beaches when they were virtually surrounded by the Germans. And, of course, we go into the British mythology of the war, this great miracle of Dunkirk. But nothing could disguise the fact that it was a terrible military defeat. The British had been driven off the continent, the French army was in shambles, and Britain had left all of its military hardware, its supplies, its materiel, on the beaches at Dunkirk. Then the Germans turned south and marched toward Paris.

On June 22, 1940, barely a month after the hostilities had actually begun, France surrendered. It was a shock of enormous proportions. Everyone around the world—military experts, intelligence experts, political figures—all had counted on the French army providing the same sort of heroic resistance that it had performed during the Great War of 1914–1918. And now, this army, this country which had stood heroically against the Germans all the way through four-plus years of war in the Great War, had collapsed within a month.

Hitler forced an armistice on the French to be signed in the same railroad car in which the Germans had signed the armistice in 1918. There is a very famous film—newsreel footage—that shows Hitler getting ready to go into the signing of the treaty. He's standing there dressed in his military uniform, which he wore, once the war began, all the time. He raises his leg and slaps his thigh in pure jubilation. The British got hold of this, of course, and—the British were very good at political propaganda—transformed the film so that Hitler does a little jig over the grave of France, as the British newsreels said. The Germans were the masters of the European continent. The British refused to see reason, as Hitler put it; refused to come to any sort of agreement. One of Hitler's worst nightmares occurred on the very day that Germany invaded in the West back in May, and that is that Neville Chamberlain stepped down, and he was replaced in office as prime minister by Winston Churchill.

Churchill had been virtually alone in Britain, considered a troublemaker, a warmonger, during the '30s for complaining about the Nazis, saying they were a danger, we're going to have to face them one of these days. He was opposed to much of the British policy of appeasement, and now Churchill was in charge of British policy. For Hitler, this was, in a way, the final straw; there would be no coming to terms with this warmonger, as Hitler liked to call him. Britain refused, in other words, to see reason, Hitler believed, and continued to fight. What ensued would be an air battle over the English Channel, and the Germans began drawing up plans for something called Operation Sea Lion, an invasion of England. There had been no plans for this. The army had had no contingency plans, there were no logistical plans that had been made, and Hitler turns to his military advisors and says, "We want to be able to invade England within six weeks."

The cross-channel invasion that the Western Allies launched against Germany on the sixth of June 1944 had taken over half a year of preparation, indeed longer. Needless to say, the German military couldn't come up with something that would work. But the prerequisite for any sort of invasion operation was achieving air superiority over the Channel, and so a month-long air battle was fought between the *Luftwaffe*, the German air force, and the RAF, called the Battle of Britain, in which the British were able to frustrate the Germans.

The Germans were not able to establish the necessary air superiority, and Hitler—although the bombing of Britain would continue and it moved over from establishing air superiority over the channel, its objective moved over to a systematic bombing of London and then later other major cities in Britain—Hitler was impatient. This wasn't the war he intended to fight. He didn't want to be at war with the English. This wasn't supposed to happen, and only because the British wouldn't see reason was he compelled to at least stay in the conflict. But as soon as there were serious objections raised to the prospects of a successful invasion, he was already ready to turn his attention away. The war against England, and the planning for it, was done at, to use the German phrase, *mit der linken hand*, "with the left hand"; it was not Hitler's primary objective, and he quickly lost patience.

He already began in the summer of 1940—while the bombing was still going on, the air battle still raging—Hitler already began to instruct his military to begin thinking about the possibilities of an invasion of the Soviet Union. In December, the high command of the army began very serious preparations for an operation called Operation Barbarossa, named after the German emperor of the Middle Ages who had driven into the east to establish territory for the German empire. For Hitler, the war against the Soviet Union had always been the main event. Nazi ideology held the Soviet Union, as we've seen over and over again, to be the center of global Judeo-Bolshevik conspiracy. Thus, war against the Soviet Union would not only have geopolitical objectives—the seizing of territory, providing the German nation with living space—but it was also a major ideological goal as well. This would be a crusade against Judeo-

Bolshevism, to save Western civilization, as Hitler put it, from this great threat.

Hitler was also convinced of two things. One was that, although Germany had been unable to invade Great Britain, and the British were still holding out, that this really wouldn't be a two-front war. Britain was eliminated as a power factor in Europe. It's true the English were holding on, but the only way that Britain could possibly play a significant role henceforth would be if somehow the United States entered the war. That's the only way Britain could prevail. They might survive, but couldn't prevail, unless for some reason the United States entered the war on Britain's side. Therefore, a turn to the east wouldn't be committing the sin of a two-front war.

He also believed, as did his military men, that the purges of the Red Army in 1938 had devastated the command structure. The Red Army was weak. He was able to draw on the Soviet experience from the Soviet invasion of Finland in late 1939 and into 1940. The Soviet Union had invaded Finland with almost disastrous results; the tiny Finnish army had fought a winter war, frustrating the Red Army, holding out, putting up their tremendous struggle. The Red Army did not look like a serious military force. Hitler believed that the Red Army—and the Soviet Union, more broadly—were rotten to the core. One only had to kick in the door, Hitler said, and the whole rotten structure would collapse within a matter of weeks.

In late summer of 1940, then, Hitler shifted his attention to the east and despite the non-aggression pact with Stalin, had begun planning for an invasion of the Soviet Union. This was to be ideological war to the death; Hitler warned his generals that this was not going to be a war like the war against France or against England—that this was a war to be fought with unusual rules beyond the traditional practices of warfare. His top military commanders were issued an order, which came to be known as the "Commissar Order." That order was followed by a series of other directives, which gave a very clear indication of how different this war in the east would be. Let me read you a passage from this Commissar Order. This was to be read to the troops invading the Soviet Union:

"In the struggle against Bolshevism, we must not assume that the enemy's conduct will be based on principles of humanity or of international law. In particular, hateful, cruel, and inhuman treatment of our prisoners is to be expected from political commissars of all kinds, as the real carriers of resistance" (meaning commissars of the Bolshevik Party). "The troops must be advised: 1) in this struggle, consideration and respect for International Law with regard to these elements are wrong. They are a danger for our own security and for the rapid pacification of conquered territory. The originators of barbaric Asiatic methods of warfare are the political commissars of the Bolshevik Party. Accordingly, measures must be taken against them immediately and with full severity. Accordingly, whether captured in battle, or offering resistance, they are, in principle, to be disposed of by arms."

In case this message wasn't clear, a set of guidelines was issued to the troops. Those guidelines stated quite clearly: "1) Bolshevism is the mortal enemy of the National Socialist German people. Germany's struggle is directed against this destructive ideology and its carriers. This struggle demands ruthless and energetic measures against Bolshevik agitators, guerrillas, saboteurs, Jews, and the complete elimination of every active or passive resistance." I emphasize this list: Bolsheviks, Bolshevik agitators, guerrillas, saboteurs, Jews. It goes without saying that Bolshevik agitators were not going to be very easy to round up; saboteurs, the same; guerrillas, the same. But the Jewish community of what had been Eastern Poland and Western Russia would become obvious targets. So, in this list of people to be eliminated wherever they were found—this was issued to the troops.

Following up those directives, another statement was issued to the troops. The most essential aim of the campaign, and I quote, "against the Jewish Bolshevist system is the complete crushing of its means of power and the extermination of Asiatic influences in the European region. This poses tasks for the troops that go beyond the one-sided routine of conventional soldering in the eastern region. The soldier is not merely a fighter, according to the rules of the art of war, but also the bearer of an inexorable national idea, and the avenger of all bestialities inflicted upon the German people and its racial kin. Therefore, the soldier must have full understanding for the necessity of a severe but just revenge on Jewish sub-humanity. An additional aim in this is to nip in the bud any revolts in the rear of the army, which, as experience proves, have always been instigated by Jews."

An additional order made it quite clear to the commanders and to the troops in the field that actions taken that in the past would have been subject to military law, to court martial—things that might have been considered atrocities—would not be considered atrocities in this instance, that there would be no legal repercussions for actions taken in this extraordinary theater of warfare. In addition, special SS commando units, the *Einsatzgruppen*, they were called, would accompany the troops into the Soviet Union and would be given "special tasks."

These *Einsatzgruppen* had been given similar special tasks in Poland during the invasion of Poland in September of 1939, where they moved in alongside the troops and rounded up members of the Jewish community—committed all sorts of atrocities, to the shock of the military commanders and to the German troops. There were a lot of complaints during the Polish campaign, emanating from the German high command and from German troops in the ground, that these SS commando units were getting in the way of military operations. What were they doing out there? They were just increasing resistance by stirring up Polish resistance, with their violent actions against Polish civilians.

But the army was told in no uncertain terms, before the invasion of the Soviet Union, that these SS commando units, the *Einsatzgruppen*, had been given their orders for special activities from the highest levels of the German government, meaning Hitler. The SS had committed itself not to get in the way. They would not interfere with military operations, but the army also should make way for them and try not to interfere with their operations either.

Troops began moving across the continent in the summer and spring of 1941: millions of men, horses, all sorts of tanks, planes, artillery pieces. The original date for the invasion had been set for the spring of 1941, as soon as the spring rains stopped, but the weather didn't cooperate. It was one of the rainiest springs in 20th-century European history, which made the terrain in Eastern Poland and in the Soviet Union beyond difficult to negotiate, especially for tanks. So the military thought about the possibilities of postponing it, and also Mussolini's misadventures in Greece and finally Yugoslavia meant that Germany sent troops to the south, into Yugoslavia and ultimately into Greece, in the spring, postponing the invasion date— the jump-off date—for Operation Barbarossa until late June. It would be a costly postponement.

On June 22, 1941, the Germans launched Operation Barbarossa. It was the largest military operation in human history. "The world," Hitler said, "will hold its breath." It was 129 years to the day after Napoleon's armies invaded Russia in 1812. Hitler always had a fine sense of history, but one might think that he might have been a little more cautious about choosing this particular date. In the first 48 hours, the Germans enjoyed unparalleled success. They caught the Russian troops completely unprepared, completely by surprise. They overran the initial Red Army positions; the entire Soviet air force was destroyed in 48 hours, almost all of it on the ground, so that the Soviets' Red Army operated without any sort of air cover, any significant air cover, in these operations.

The Germans, within a matter of days, drove deep into the Soviet Union. There were three army groups: the Northern Group, pressing toward Leningrad; Army Group Center, pressing toward Moscow; and Army Group South, which was headed in the direction of Kiev. I think it's important to point something out; we tend to always talk about—and I've just done it—which is to give geographic aims: Leningrad, Moscow, Kiev. But in fact, all military missions have a stated objective, and this one did, too. The real objective of Operation Barbarossa was to destroy the Red Army in Western Russia within 3–6 weeks. Then the move on Moscow would take place against very little resistance. There would be chaos. Hitler was convinced, and the military people too, that the Soviet Union would simply crumble and that the Germans would be able then to move on.

The Soviets in these first weeks of Operation Barbarossa—indeed, in the first months, June, into July, into August, into September— suffered absolutely staggering casualties. Hundreds of thousands dying in a number of huge battles—encirclement battles, where the *Blitzkrieg* seemed to be working as if it were drawn up on the boards back at German military headquarters. Hundreds of prisoners of war taken—100,000, 200,000, 300,000 prisoners of war taken as the Red Army seemed to be on the verge of collapse. And in those first few heady days—first few weeks, indeed, of the invasion—the German commander, General Halder, in charge of the whole operation, had written in his diary, "It would not be too much," he said, "to say that the Soviet Union lost the war in the first 48 hours of the conflict." A month into the invasion, again, "The Soviets have lost; it's only a matter of time," and went on to talk about possibilities of pacification of the countryside.

Indeed, in early October, Hitler ordered the German economy back on a peacetime footing. No winter gear was issued to the German military in the invasion. It was supposed to be over in six weeks. But as the summer dragged on, and the Soviets were defeated, it was clear to everybody—all in the West, the observers, the Germans thinking about it—everybody seemed to know this except the Soviets. And the Red Army, though suffering unbelievable casualties and giving up terrain by the tens and twenties of miles per day, hadn't given up. In fact, huge pockets of resistance remained behind German lines, and the Germans were suffering casualties—lots of casualties—themselves.

And as German lines moved deeper into the Soviet Union, it became more and more difficult to have their supplies reach them. The roads on the German maps of the Soviet Union—nice roads; they were no Autobahn, of course—but what looked like primary roads, big major roads, turned out to be barely paved, narrow roadways. Other secondary roads turned out to be dirt paths, so that in the fall, the fall rains started, and the Germans bogged down. One often thinks about it being general winter, as they always say—the snows and the cold weather coming—that was so devastating to Operation Barbarossa, but it had already slowed by the late summer. And one begins to get this awful sense creeping into the German military communiqués about, what's going on here? They're beaten, but they continue to resist, and we're suffering casualties, and we're short of supplies.

Germany now found itself, in the fall of 1941, trying to determine what its objective should be. It had already failed in its first objective—the destruction of the Red Army and Western Russia within six weeks. October brought the first frosts, and the ground hardened again, so the Germans thought, "We can make it forward. The tanks can roll on this terrain." And it was decided to push toward Moscow, an all-out push toward Moscow. This push began in the fall, but by this time, the Germans had lost about half of the tanks they'd begun the campaign with, not simply to Russian resistance, but just from maintenance problems.

A decision was made by Hitler to issue no winter gear. It finally had been brought up in November, when it was clear that they were still fighting. Hitler was afraid that if he issued an order for the requisition of winter gear, that this would send a signal back to the German population that the war in the Soviet Union was not going to be over in a short period of time at all; that victory wasn't within sight, that there was going to be a winter campaign—and so he refused.

In late November, early December 1941, temperatures on the eastern front dropped below zero Fahrenheit. German military vehicles froze. They hadn't brought enough antifreeze; in some cases brought none. The tank treads wouldn't function in the cold. The machines began to break down, and German troops were wearing summer denim uniforms, lightweight uniforms, in temperatures that were below zero. In these circumstances, on December 5–6, 1941, the Russians caught the Germans completely by surprise and launched a massive counterattack before Moscow. German forward units reached—there's a lot of talk about German troops actually seeing the spires of the Kremlin, but this is not actually the case; maybe a scouting patrol did at one point. But Moscow was in danger. But this counteroffensive by the Red Army on December 5–6 halted the German advance. It halted the *Blitzkrieg* phase of the war, making clear to Hitler and to his high command that the long war of attrition, which they had so greatly feared, was upon them.

Then, on December 7, 1941, all the way across the world, the Japanese attack on Pearl Harbor brought the United States into the conflict. Germany and Japan had a very, very loose sort of agreement of mutual support. The Japanese had certainly done nothing to support the Germans to this point, and the Germans weren't aware the Japanese were going to attack. It was a surprise. But on December 11, 1941, Hitler declared war on the United States, solving Franklin Roosevelt's domestic problem, since the American public was certainly ready to go to war against Japan. But now, what had been a European war and an Asian war merged into one—something that was truly a world war.

Lecture Eleven
Holocaust—Hitler's War Against the Jews

Scope:

The war, and especially the murderous conflict in the east, fundamentally changed the problems and possibilities of Nazi racial policy. In this lecture, we will trace the radicalization of Nazi Jewish policy between 1939 and 1945, tracing the steps and considerations that led from a policy of expulsion to one of mass murder. We will examine the organizations and individuals charged with shaping that policy, especially the SS, the Central Security Office (*Reichssicherheitshauptamt*), Heinrich Himmler, and Reinhard Heydrich. Between 1939 and 1942, the Nazis pursued several options in attempting to solve what they referred to as "the Jewish question": the "Jewish reservation system," the Madagascar Plan, and a campaign of massive pogroms on the eastern front, among others.

Outline

I. The evolution of Nazi racial policy, 1939–1941.

    A. The invasion of Poland in 1939 and the subsequent invasion of the Soviet Union in the summer of 1941 put the Nazis in control of Europe's largest Jewish communities and required, the Nazis believed, a new policy.

    B. Hitler placed responsibility for finding a "solution to the Jewish question" in the hands of Reichsführer SS Heinrich Himmler.

    C. Already in 1939, the Nazis created the Government General of Poland, an area of Polish territory not annexed outright to Germany. The Government General was to be a "dumping ground" for Jews who were already being rounded up in Czechoslovakia and Austria for "resettlement" by October 1939. In 1940, the deportation of Western European Jews to the Government General began.

    D. The head of the Nazi government in the Government General complained that the situation there was becoming impossible; a new solution had to be found.

E. Himmler delegated Reinhard Heydrich, head of the Reich Security Office, to develop "a final solution" to the Jewish problem.

II. During 1940–1941, the Nazi leadership considered several options.

   A. The regime also entertained a proposal to create a "Jewish reservation system" somewhere in the east, possibly beyond the Urals.

   B. The regime briefly considered using the concentration camp system in Germany—Buchenwald, Dachau, Sachsenhausen, and the others—to imprison Jews but quickly dismissed the idea.

   C. Meanwhile, the *Einsatzgruppen* (special SS units) were given responsibility for rounding up Jews and placing them in ghettos.

   D. Though the Nazis had played on popular anti-Semitic sentiments, their racism was far broader in scope, potentially including anyone of non-Aryan background.

   E. More consideration was given to the so-called Madagascar Plan, which called for the deportation of all European Jews to the French colony of Madagascar; French Prime Minister Pierre Laval was more than agreeable.

III. Later developments.

   A. Euphemistic terminology, such as "the final solution," was regularly used to describe the extermination of Jews.

      1. In 1939, a euthanasia program was initiated to institute "racial hygiene" in Germany. Children (and later adults) with abnormalities, handicaps, or learning disabilities were labeled as "racially valueless."

      2. Some 5,000 children and 80,000 to 100,000 adults were killed.

      3. Hitler avoided any direct responsibility for the program.

   B. While these plans were under considerable criticism, the SS commando units (*Einsatzgruppen*) were murdering Jews by the thousands on the eastern front in what seemed a massive pogrom.

   C. Heydrich considered all these solutions and dismissed each of them.

D. In particular, the actions of the *Einsatzgruppen* were too public (too many German soldiers witnessed these massacres), too unruly, and too inefficient. Although the eastern policy was never overtly announced, the Germans hardly concealed the facts from their own troops and the local population.

E. In the summer of 1941, Himmler received a direct order from Hitler to find a permanent solution to the "Jewish problem."

F. By 1941, information about the massive pogrom on the eastern front had reached the Allies. Given their tenuous military situation, however, they were in no position to intervene.

Essential Reading:

Friedländer, Henry, *The Origins of Nazi Genocide*.

Browning, Christopher, *Ordinary Men*.

Levi, Primo, *Survival in Auschwitz*.

Supplementary Reading:

Breitman, Richard, *The Architect of Genocide: Himmler and the Final Solution* and *Official Secrets: What the Nazis Planned, What the British and Americans Knew*.

Goldhagen, Daniel, *Hitler's Willing Executioners*.

Kershaw, Ian, *The Nazi Dictatorship*.

Kogon, Eugen, *The Theory and Practice of Hell*.

Questions to Consider:

1. Was the Holocaust the result of long-term trends in German political culture that were simply waiting for release or a product of a deviant Nazi ideology and the "radicalizing" decision-making process in the Third Reich?

2. Was the Nazi genocide the result of an ideological blueprint that Hitler had envisioned since early in his career or more an ideologically conditioned product of improvisation and circumstance?

Lecture Eleven—Transcript
Holocaust—Hitler's War Against the Jews

Hello, and welcome to our eleventh lecture in our series on the history of Hitler's empire. In our last lecture, we examined the German invasion of the Soviet Union in 1941 and concluded with the Russian counteroffensive before Moscow in December. That victory of the Russians holding before Moscow, of course, could mark a turning point in the war, as indeed it did. It halted the *Blitzkrieg* phase of the conflict. It certainly made quite clear to the Germans that they were in for the long war of attrition which Hitler hoped to avoid, and Hitler's announcement of declaration of war against the United States, four days later on December 11, 1941, made this war—a European war—now a global war.

One of the reasons for Hitler's doing that, I should say, to close off that discussion from our last session, was that his naval commanders had been lobbying for quite some time for Hitler to allow them to attack American shipping. The United States, on the Lend-Lease program, had been shipping materiel and supplies to Great Britain for some time. German submarines were sitting out in the mid-Atlantic, and were telling Hitler, "We're already at war with the United States. We can sink ships by the ton if you only would give us the green light to go ahead." The Japanese attack on Pearl Harbor on December 7, naval commanders believed, would occupy American attention—that's where most American naval strength would be located—and the German submarines would have a field day.

Also, Hitler and his advisers simply did not take the United States seriously as a military power. At the time that Hitler declared war, the United States still had an army that was smaller than France's had been in 1940. There was no reason to anticipate, also, that the United States would be able to transform a peacetime economy, a consumer economy, into a wartime economy on the scale that it did. In fact, it would be one of the great miracles of the Second World War, this American economic expansion. These topics and indeed all the topics that we will discuss very briefly here about the Second World War are dealt with far more extensively in our course on the Second World War, which is available also through the Teaching Company.

The war against the Soviet Union, we saw, had ideological objectives as well as geopolitical objectives. It was the crusade against Judeo-Bolshevism, and indeed, the war in the east had already become something else besides a military campaign. It was the onset of racial war. It was a war against the Jews. Hitler had made a statement in 1939, on January 30, on the sixth anniversary of his seizure of power. He made this in front of the Reichstag, so it was covered over the radio, covered in the international press. I'd like to quote it; this is of course before the war begins:

"One more thing I would like now to state on this day, memorable perhaps not only for us Germans: I have often been called a prophet in my life, and was generally laughed at. During my struggle for power, the Jews primarily received with laughter my prophecies that I would someday assume the leadership of the State, and thereby of the entire *volk*, and then, among other things, achieve a solution to the Jewish problem. I suppose that meanwhile, then resounding laughter of Jewry in Germany is now choking in their throats. Today I will be a prophet again. If international financed Jewry within Europe and abroad should succeed once more in plunging the peoples into a world war, then the consequence will be, not be the Bolshevization of the world, and therefore victory of Jewry, but on the contrary, the destruction of the Jewish race in Europe!"

The invasion of Poland in 1939, and the Soviet Union two years later, of course, put Germany in control of Europe's largest Jewish communities. In October 1939, Heinrich Himmler was named Reich commissar for the strengthening of German *volkdom*, a new title that gave him responsibility for National Socialist racial policy in the occupied territories. Himmler delegated that authority to Reinhard Heydrich in a so-called Reich Security Central Office, where SS specialists were already at work on finding a solution to the so-called "Jewish question." Immigration, the policy of prewar Germany, would now become expulsion.

In a memorandum drafted on September 19,1939, entitled *The Jewish Question in the Occupied Territories*, Heydrich laid out the foundations of National Socialist policy. In those territories annexed to Germany—that is, those areas of old Czechoslovakia or Poland, it would be outright annexed and would become part of the *Gross Deutsche Reich*. All non-Germans were to be expelled; those territories would be cleansed of all so-called non-Aryan elements, in preparation for future settlement by Germans. This meant evacuating all Slavs and Jews to an area, a new state, created on October 12, 1939 as a kind of dumping ground for Jews, Poles, and others coming out of German territory. This was the so-called Government General of Poland. Moreover, all Jews were to be rounded up and concentrated in a few selected urban areas in this Government General.

Indeed, Himmler's September 19 memorandum suggests that this ghettoization was not the final aim, but represented an intermediate step. These concentration centers, or ghettos, were to be located near major rail centers, hinting that further transport was being considered. It was at this time as well that the idea of a Jewish reservation—somewhere in the Lublin district or perhaps farther east—was openly discussed as a possible solution. There had been some discussion about using the concentration camps within Germany itself—Dachau, Buchenwald, Sachsenhausen and so on— but that was rejected. The large Jewish population was in Eastern Europe; the Nazis did not want to be moving Jews from Eastern Europe into the heartland of Germany. It would be too public, too visible, and logistically more difficult. So that had been rejected.

The reservation idea was a possibility. Responsibility for executing this policy was placed in the hands of special SS units, *Einsatzgruppen*, that we've talked about, who had been developed for the invasion of Poland. These were men with special training, indoctrination of Nazi racial policy; they numbered about 3,000. It is estimated that approximately 1 million people were rounded up and forced into the ghettos in the Government General in 1939 into 1940. In fact, by October 1939, the SS began the deportation of Jews from Austria and Czechoslovakia to the Government General, and in a signal of radical National Socialist racial thinking, so-called Aryan children were selected for resettlement in Germany.

This was a hint, I think, as one looks at SS thinking about this. This would be a program that would be developed and kept in place all the way through the war. Children who had so-called Aryan features—they were blond-headed, blue-eyed, tall, slender—were to be taken away from their parents, also young women, and brought back to Germany, where they were to be raised in special SS homes, or bred with SS men, in the case of the young women. What one sees already in this action is a very important distinction, and one worth underscoring. Certainly, the Nazis had played on popular anti-Semitism in their rise to power, and anti-Semitism was still the driving force within National Socialism. But in fact, Nazi racism was far broader than anti-Semitism.

The term that Germans use for Germans is *deutsche*; the Nazis would often use *germanen*; Germanics, I suppose, would be an awkward English translation; and then, of course, *arierin*, Aryans. These three things were not the same thing. In the kind of never-never land of SS thinking, Aryans were to be found in all of the different populations of Europe. These were the special racial elements that had to be selected out wherever they found them in Poland, in Czechoslovakia, in Russia, so that they could be part of the creation of what was called a master race, a *herrenvolk*. It wasn't the Germans, *die deutsche*, who were that master race, though this is what the Nazis implied in all of their propaganda to the German population. Rather, the Germans were, the SS believed, the last, best racial hope of humanity, the least spoiled, the least contaminated. But it was their job to find these specimens of racial purity wherever German troops went.

Problems with the various schemes emerged relatively quickly. As we saw, the army high command was appalled at the sheer brutality of the *Einsatzgruppen* in Poland in 1939, who moved right in behind the Wehrmacht troops, and led to complaints to various National Socialist officials, including Himmler and Hitler. We talked about this with the invasion of the Soviet Union; the *Einsatzgruppen*'s relationship with the army would be rather different. But as the war continued in 1940 and went into the West, Hans Frank, the Nazi official in charge of the Government General, complained bitterly that the Government General was, in fact, being reduced to little more than a dumping ground for all of Europe's Jews and undesirables. It was going to become a hotbed of disease. If more and more people were being transported into this small area of prewar Poland, he wasn't going to be able to master the situation.

Indeed, by October 1940, Jews were being deported from Western Europe to the Government General. It was at this point that Himmler ordered the construction of a camp at Auschwitz to handle the overflow of Jews being brought into the Government General. The SS considered several options at this point. In February 1940, the Jewish reservation idea seems to have been approved by Goering, by

Himmler, and Frank, but was dropped less than a month later. There were problems with the idea of this Jewish reservation. First of all, where would it be? Ultimately, after the invasion of the Soviet Union, the idea popped up again, and maybe the idea of a Jewish reservation somewhere out beyond the Urals, off at the edge of civilization, as they liked to put it. That was a problem, and there were certainly no more options left in Poland, the Nazis felt; at least Hans Frank didn't feel so.

At roughly the same time, another plan was put forward within the SS that had been discussed off and on since the outbreak of the war. That was the idea of settling Europe's Jews somewhere in Africa. In fact, the place that was chosen was the French island colony of Madagascar. In May 1940, Himmler wrote a memo to Hitler on the "treatment of foreign nationals in the east," in which he stated, "I hope to see the concept of Jews completely obliterated, with the possibility of a large migration of all Jews to Africa, or else to a colony." Pierre Laval, the French premier at this point, and a collaborationist of the first degree, was actively offering Madagascar as a place to resettle Europe's Jews.

Certainly, the SS and especially the Reich Security Central Office under Heydrich, drafted numerous memoranda on issues of international law, transport, etc., in pursuance of this Madagascar option. But as 1940 turned to 1941, no solution had been found, and confusion reigned in National Socialist policy. Again, this problem that we referred to earlier, of taking a general ideological directive— it was clear that Hitler was talking about the elimination of the Jews, but what exactly did that mean? Did it mean a reservation somewhere out in the east? Did it mean a Madagascar Plan, as this was now called? What exactly did it mean? How did you translate that desire into a specific policy?

While these policy options were being discussed in top secret within the Reich Security Central Office, another set of decisions in another area of policy—apparently unrelated to events in Poland or Jewish policy—took form, that would come to play an ominously central role in the evolution of what came to be called as the "final solution" to the Jewish problem. Indeed, this is the terminology that was used. The SS and the Nazis always proceeded with euphemistic terminology. So it all, in discussing the so-called Jewish problem or the Jewish question, they would always talk about a "final solution," *endlösung*, to this issue. But far away from Poland, as I said, developments were occurring which would play an important and terrible role in that ultimate "final solution."

In 1939, the Nazis had initiated a program, a euthanasia program, in Germany itself. It was directed by men named Philipp Bouhler and Dr. Karl Brandt, and it worked out of Hitler's chancellery in Berlin. This was in pursuance of what the Nazis called racial hygiene: to cleanse the *volkskorp*, or the body of the people, of all bacteria, of all elements that might weaken the health of the *volksgemeinschaft*, the people's community. In pursuance of this, Brandt and Bouhler set up 21 special children's departments in hospitals around the country to evaluate children with birth defects, with any sort of physical abnormality, children who were mentally retarded or had some other sort of learning disability. To identify them, they used social agencies, including of the church, to identify children with these learning disabilities and so on, without explaining what exactly was at stake in this.

Part of this was the Nazis were obsessed with—they talked about—public health. How does one restore public health, create a healthy people's community, a healthy body for the people? Within SS circles, however, they talked about these children as "racially valueless" children. The German term is as ghastly as the English; it's *lebensunwertes leben*, literally meaning "life unworthy of life." Dr. Leonardo Conti, who was appointed head of this program, was very eager to take part, but this is a very interesting point: Dr. Conti wanted to have a written authorization from Hitler himself before he would sign on to be the head of this program to remove the "racially valueless" children—and what remove meant was to kill. It is very, very typical and very, very significant that Hitler refused—and Conti resigned.

Hitler himself was always interested in what we would now call deniability. He didn't want to be directly associated with this. Part of the reason for that, and other less sinister projects, was that if it didn't work, if a policy didn't work, he could distance himself from it. It was the fault of the person who initiated it, who ran it, not his. But in this, Hitler didn't want to have anything to do with a written document associating him with this plan. Nonetheless, the plan went forward. In 1940, the program expanded to cover adults who were currently housed in asylums; people with various handicaps, mental as well as physical; people with social problems, meaning alcoholics, chronic alcoholics. Still run out of now Bouhler's office in the Reich Chancellery, the personnel for this program were drawn from the SS, and six euthanasia installations were established around the country.

The children, and then later the adults, were to be killed by injection. But in 1939, the first experiments were conducted within this euthanasia program with poison gas; 20–30 patients were taken to special shower stalls and gassed as part of this program. The parents of the children, the relatives of the adults who were killed in this fashion, received what looked like personal letters, but were in fact form letters, saying "Your son/your daughter/your brother/your husband/your wife has died of complications from an operation or from disease." No explanation. Over 5,000 "racially valueless" children, as the Nazis put it, died in this euthanasia program in this period; 80,000–100,000 mentally defective or handicapped adults also fell victim to Nazi racial hygiene, as they called it.

At one point in August of 1941, the veil of secrecy, which they were determined to keep, slipped a little bit, and there was actually a protest of several mothers who discovered, quite by accident, that they had all gotten the same sort of letter about what had happened to their children, and they demanded some sort of explanation; they went public with it. The program backed off; the murders were halted temporarily, but after a brief pause would pick up once again. It's a broader notion of race—of cleansing the racial stock of the country. In August of 1941, of course, German troops were now deep inside the Soviet Union, and indeed, the war against the Soviet Union would profoundly affect Nazi racial policy.

We already have cited the infamous Commissar Order—the order to kill partisan saboteurs, Bolshevik commissars, and Jews—clearly indicated that the war against the Soviet Union was also to be a war against Bolshevism and world Jewry. The mistakes of the Polish campaign were to be avoided here; there would be no sources of friction between the army and the SS. This was important, because Reinhard Heydrich had assembled four *Einsatzgruppen* to move into the Soviet Union along with the troops. They were to conduct "special operations" and to report not to the local military authorities, along whom they would be working side by side, but rather directly to the Reich Führer SS, or to the Reich Sicherheit Hauptamt, the Reich Central Security Office headed by Heydrich. The SS engaged in mass shootings of Jews, partisans, and what they called Slavic *untermenchen*, sub-humans. Indeed, the *Einsatzgruppen* conducted a bloodbath all over the eastern front in September–October of 1941. A report of December 1941 by SS Colonel Yaeger, who headed a commando in *Einsatzgruppa* A, described the procedures used by his group, but they're typical of all. Let me quote:

"The decision to free each district of Jews necessitated thorough preparation of each action as well as acquisition of information about local conditions. The Jews had to be collected in one or more towns, and a ditch had to be dug at the right site for the right number. The marching distance from collecting points to the ditches averaged about three miles. The Jews were brought in groups of 500, separated by at least 1.2 miles, to the place of execution. The sort of difficulties and nerve-wracking work involved in this is shown by an arbitrarily chosen example. In Rokiskis, 3,208 people had to be transported three miles before they could be liquidated. Vehicles are seldom available. Distances to and from actions were never less than 90 to 120 miles. Only careful planning enabled the commandos to carry out up to five actions a week, and at the same time continue the work in Kovno without interruption. In Kovno itself, where trained Lithuanian volunteers are available in sufficient numbers, this, comparatively speaking, is shooting paradise."

Not only could the SS count on their own trained personnel, but also on locals, who, in the Baltic states in particular, were more than willing to participate in these pogroms, as well as in certain areas of Poland, Ukraine, and so on.

For Himmler and for Heydrich, there were problems, however, in this system. For one thing, they were too public, and they were too sloppy. Heydrich, who was after all in charge of racial policy in the occupied territories in the east, was particularly disturbed. The shootings could not be concealed from the German troops, and in many cases German troops participated, thinking they were supposed to. Nobody quite understood. Some units would be involved because they didn't understand that there was a distinction between these SS commando units and their own. Their local commanders didn't and so they might participate. But mostly, they didn't.

However, in the early stages of the campaign in the Soviet Union, soldiers who had cameras—were taking cameras with them during Operation Barbarossa—would take pictures. Often you will see very terrifying photographs, and they'll be of several German soldiers, obviously at a break, during a break in the fighting, relaxing. They'll have their arms around each other and maybe a bottle of vodka in one hand, and they are laughing and clearly relaxed. But if you look at the photograph carefully, in the background, what do you see? You see a line of people—Jews—with a ditch in front of them, or you see someone about to be shot, or you see—there's several photographs that were brought back where these SS commandos were burning the beard of an orthodox Jew, or humiliating them in one form or another.

These photographs went back to Germany. People knew about it; people found out about this. There was never any announcement that this was policy—that these commando units were operating this way in the Soviet Union. But the Germans didn't do a great deal to conceal this, either; that is, from their own troops, and certainly not from the local population. This was something that the Nazis, that Heydrich, would argue was important. It was not only important the troops have a limited knowledge and the population at home a limited knowledge of this, they also had to maintain the ignorance of the potential victims. If word got out about how this was operating, then there would be serious resistance. There was resistance by the Jewish community in various places, but against overwhelming force.

Also, this was just too inefficient: marching people, places, taking up time, having ditches dug, shooting, unbelievably inhumane, grisly terrifying actions which had now become commonplace in the eastern front. This, Heydrich believed, did have to be kept secret. It had to be kept secret from the Allies, who would make great propaganda out of it, and the photographs being sent home stopped too. German censors began to monitor this much more carefully. No, some sort of "final solution" had to be found—and this was Heydrich's job—some way to streamline the business of murder.

As a consequence, Heydrich began working on this sometime in the summer of 1941. They had gone through various possibilities, as we've seen. But it really is clear that at some point in the summer of 1941, when the Nazis thought they were winning the war in the Soviet Union, when the horizon of possibility now seemed limitless, at some point in that summer, Himmler received a direct order from Hitler. Not a written order—deniability again—but a nod. All that it would have taken would have been a nod from Hitler for Himmler to know what this meant. Faced with the options available, some sort of other solution needed to be adopted, a solution that would allow the SS to proceed in this policy without a prying world looking on.

Several years ago, a very distinguished historian whom I respect a great deal, named Richard Breitman, published a book about what the Allies knew, what the German population knew, and so on. It was picked up, excerpts picked up by *The New York Times* as blockbuster news that, in fact, after looking through (using the Freedom of Information Act) cables from Britain to the United States during 1941, that the American and British governments had information about "the Holocaust." What the British and American governments had information about—information that came to them through the Polish underground, came from Jews who had escaped and made it somehow to the West—was that this bloodbath of the *Einsatzgruppen* was going on in Eastern Europe; that a massive pogrom of unimaginable proportions was being conducted on the eastern front. This the Allies knew, but were in no position to do anything about it.

In 1941, certainly the British were still hanging on, the United States not yet involved in the war, and there was a good deal of skepticism about it. There was not yet the sense that this was a methodical, large-scale program. That large-scale methodical program, "the final solution to the Jewish question," would come in January of 1942, at his top-secret conference in a Berlin suburb of Wannsee, where Reinhard Heydrich would explain to a select group of party officials just what "the final solution" to the Jewish question in Europe would be.

Lecture Twelve
The Final Solution

Scope:

In late 1941, the Third Reich finally opted for what it called "the final solution." Developed by Reinhard Heydrich, this ultimate solution called for the deportation of all Europe's Jews to specially created concentration camps in the east for "resettlement." That resettlement, however, was in reality mass murder in the gas chambers of the new death camps, such as Auschwitz and Treblinka. Between 1941 and 1945, six million to eight million Jews would perish in this holocaust. In the first week of May 1945, after Adolf Hitler had committed suicide in his bunker beneath the devastated Reich Chancellery, the war in Europe came, at last, to an end. In the concluding portion of the lecture, we turn our attention to the lessons that the experience of the Third Reich offers us today.

Outline

I. "The final solution."

　　A. In the summer of 1941, Heydrich, acting on an oral order from Hitler, began drafting his own solution. There appears to be no written document linking Hitler to the plan, but he almost never committed himself to paper anyway. His plan called for:

　　　　1. The creation of a new concentration camp system in the east.

　　　　2. The deportation of all European Jews to these camps for "resettlement."

　　　　3. The construction in these new camps of special gassing installations, because, in fact, "resettlement" meant mass extermination of European Jews.

　　B. Heydrich called a secret meeting of a small group of party and state officials for January 20, 1942, in the Berlin suburb of Wannsee to announce his plan.

　　　　1. Heydrich was the ranking official present—Hitler, Himmler, Goebbels, and other top officials, though informed of the meeting, were not participants. The subject under discussion was the "resettlement"—or

physical extermination—of all European Jews. The meeting lasted little more than an hour.

   2. Death camps would be established in Poland, Czechoslovakia, and elsewhere to handle this massive operation. The "unfit" would be marched directly to the gas chambers. This was to be the "final solution."

   3. Heydrich emphasized the need for secrecy because the German public was not ready for this sort of extreme action, the Allies would make great propaganda out of it, and the victims must be ignorant of the fate awaiting them at the end of the train journey.

C. Implementation of the "final solution" began in the spring of 1942.

   1. Auschwitz, Treblinka, and the other death camps (*Vernichtungslager*) gradually expanded their operations.

   2. Deportations from the Warsaw ghetto began on July 22, 1942, to Treblinka.

   3. Many people arrived in cattle cars. Those selected for immediate death were told they would be taking a "shower" after a difficult journey. In a bunker-like shower room, they were crammed together, one person per square foot, and the door was shut. Once the poison gas filtered in, the dying took anywhere from 10 to 30 minutes.

   4. Anything of value from the bodies was claimed.

   5. From 1942 to 1945, it is estimated that four million to five million victims were killed by gassing, while over a million more died in the operations of the *Einsatzgruppen*.

   6. Russians, Poles, gypsies, and others also disappeared into the ovens.

II. The Allied response to the camps.

A. Not until 1944 did hard information on the camps become available to the Allies.

B. In August of 1944, the Allies bombed the general area of Buchenwald. A debate raged over whether to attack the camps, however, given that many inmates would unavoidably be killed in such an action.

C. The Allies finally decided that the best way to save lives was to attack the Nazi war machine—not the camps—and to destroy it as quickly as possible.

III. On the military front, 1942–1943 brought the turning point.

    A. Germany suffered two decisive defeats.

        1. The titanic battle fought at Stalingrad between October 1942 and February 1943 ended with a complete German defeat; the battle marked the turning point in the war in the east.

        2. In November 1942, the Western Allies launched an invasion of French North Africa, which would drive Hitler's *Afrika Korps* out of Africa by February 1943.

        3. In the spring of 1943, the Western Allies mounted an invasion of Sicily, then Italy; Germany was clearly on the defensive.

    B. The Allied air assault on Germany gathered momentum in 1943.

        1. The British firebombing of Hamburg in July set the tone for an all-out assault on German industry and urban areas.

        2. The Americans pursued a policy of "daylight precision bombing," seeking to destroy key industrial nodes.

        3. The British bombing at night and the Americans by day meant round-the-clock bombing of Germany.

IV. The drive for Germany—1944–1945.

    A. On June 6, 1944, the Western Allies invaded Normandy—D-Day.

        1. These forces liberated France by late August and moved into the Low Countries.

        2. Meanwhile, the Red Army unleashed a massive offensive in the summer of 1944 that sent its troops through Poland and to the frontier of Germany.

        3. On July 20, 1944, elements of the German army attempted to assassinate Hitler and bring down the Third Reich, but the plot was a failure.

    B. In the spring of 1945, the vise was closing on Hitler's Germany.

        1. A bold German counteroffensive in the Ardennes (the Battle of the Bulge) in December 1944 to January 1945 made impressive headway but was ultimately thwarted. It would be the last significant German offensive of the war. It was a disaster for Germany's military position.

2. The Western Allies crossed the Rhine and began to fan out over western Germany.

3. The Russians crossed the Oder and began a final push toward Berlin.

4. On April 30, Hitler committed suicide in Berlin, and on May 2, 1945, Germany surrendered; the "thousand-year" Third Reich ceased to exist after just 12 horrific years.

V. Conclusions.

A. The German people were burdened with feelings of shame and guilt.

B. Theirs is a legacy that must be shared by everyone, especially in democratic societies.

C. Let us hope that being forewarned of such horrors will make us vigilant in making sure they do not recur.

Essential Reading:

Keegan, John, *The Second World War*.

Supplementary Reading:

Trevor-Roper, Hugh, *The Last Days of Hitler*.

Speer, Albert, *Inside the Third Reich*.

Questions to Consider:

1. Could Hitler have won the Second World War? Why did the Allies prevail? What were Hitler's most critical blunders?

2. How would you evaluate the role of the Third Reich in shaping the post-war world?

3. What did the Allies know about the death camps and what could or should have been done about them?

Lecture Twelve—Transcript
The Final Solution

Hello, and welcome to the last of our lectures in this course on the history of Hitler's empire. We had concluded our last session with a discussion of Nazi thoughts, Nazi plans, Nazi options for finding what they euphemistically referred to as "the final solution" to the Jewish question in Europe. In this, our last lecture, we want to turn to that "final solution," and to the war and the final collapse of Hitler's Third Reich.

As we've seen, at some point in the summer of 1941, perhaps intoxicated by their apparent victory over the USSR, Hitler and his top advisers had come to the conclusion that some sort of "final solution to the Jewish question" was at hand, and that Hitler had issued a verbal order to seek a "final solution to the Jewish question." The date is uncertain; there certainly is no written evidence. This is one of the red herrings that has been raised sometimes by Holocaust deniers, that there is—or trying to limit somehow Hitler's responsibility—that there is no written document. David Irving, the notorious English historian, once offered a reward of several hundred pounds for anyone who could show a written document linking Hitler directly to this "final solution."

He might as well have made 10 million pounds because, as he very well knew, and everyone else who has worked on this knows, Hitler did not commit himself to paper. He did not write down words. You can go through the archives of the Third Reich, and if you find very much at all in Hitler's handwriting, it would be a remarkable find. That's why, among other things, the discovery over ten years ago—I guess it is now—of the "Hitler Diaries" was in many ways a remarkable fraud, since no one could really imagine Hitler taking time even to write down his thoughts. So no order, written order, came directly from Hitler; at least, we've never been able to find one, but it is perfectly obvious that an order was given.

On July 31, 1941, for example, Heydrich received Goering's formal authorization to prepare a total solution to the Jewish question. Goering? Why Goering? Why not Himmler? Goering, as head of the Office of the Four-Year Plan, a plan that had been charged with putting the Nazis on an economic footing to conduct the war, had become involved in Jewish matters as a result of his expropriation of Jewish property, and so Goering, in the complicated overlapping

©2001 The Teaching Company.

jurisdictions of the National Socialist Party and State, Goering would issue the authorization to prepare this "total solution," this *gesamtlösung* onto the Jewish question in Europe. The text, actually, was probably dictated by Heydrich and simply signed by Goering.

At this point, the old policy of "resettlement" was still in place for German and Western European Jews. But Heydrich, at some point in the late summer, must have come to the conclusion that the most effective course was something else. He drew on the existing policies and institutions of the Third Reich, the concentration camp system, but not the camps within Germany. These were off limits; these were for political prisoners and other undesirables and, at this point, were in the process of becoming labor camps for the German war effort. But a concentration camp system would be created somewhere else. Resettlement actually meant forced immigration; resettlement meant the transport of Europe's Jews to somewhere, to a set of camps in the east.

Finally, he drew on the experience of the *Einstazgruppen*'s activities in Russia, and the euthanasia program in Germany and their experimentation with poison gas to eliminate unhealthy undesirables in Germany, to pull together what would be his "final solution" to the Jewish question. What Heydrich was now embarked upon was a plan for the systematic mass murder of Europe's Jews.

It is clear from testimony that we have, from documents that we have, that by October, a plan to use the camps that had already been established in the Government General for mass extermination using poison gas had taken shape. In November, Hitler told one foreign office official that, "The destruction of the Jews is being planned. Now the destruction of the Jews is imminent." And, an invitation to a conference at the Berlin suburb of Wannsee was sent to state and party agencies in November of 1941 to discuss a matter of pressing urgency. This was to be a very small group to attend this conference, and it was clear that it was going to deal with the so-called Jewish problem. That conference was postponed. It was set for the first week of December 1941, but was postponed, in part because of the Russian counterattack and then the American entry into the war in early December.

It was to be held on January 20, 1942, but even beforehand, it was clear what the agenda would be. Hans Frank in the Government General, for example, sent a representative of his to Berlin to talk to

Heydrich personally to see, to ascertain, to determine for sure, what was going to be discussed at this important conference. This is what Frank reported to a number of his colleagues back in the Government General before the conference at Wannsee:

"As for the Jews, I will be quite open with you. They will have to be finished off one way or the other. The Führer said once, if the whole of Jewry once again succeeds in unleashing a world war, then peoples who have been hounded into this war will not be the only ones to shed their blood, because the Jews in Europe will meet their end. I know that many of the measures now being taken against the Jews in the Reich are criticized. It's clear from reports on popular opinion in Germany that there are accusations of cruelty and harshness. Before I continue, I would like you to agree with me in the following principle: We're only prepared to show compassion towards the German people and to no one else on earth. The others did not show compassion toward us. As an old National Socialist, I might state that if the Jewish clan were to survive the war in Europe, while we had sacrificed our best blood in the defense of Europe, then this war would only represent a partial success.

"With respect to the Jews, therefore, I will only operate on the assumption that they will disappear. They must go. I have begun negotiations with the aim of deporting them to the east. In January, there is to be a big meeting in Berlin on this question, to which I will send my representative. This meeting is to take place in the Reich Security Main Office under SS Obergruppen Führer Heydrich, his chairmanship. In any event, a big Jewish migration will begin. What will happen to the Jews? Do you imagine that they will actually be resettled in villages in the east? People said to us in Berlin, why do we go to all the trouble? We in the east or in the Ukraine do not know what to do with them either. Liquidate them yourselves, gentlemen. I must ask you to arm yourself against any feelings of compassion. We must exterminate the Jews whenever we find them and whenever it is possible to do so in order to maintain the whole structure of the Reich here.

"That will, of course, occur through methods other than those to which we are accustomed. The point is that this does not come within the framework of the legal process. One cannot apply views held up to now to such gigantic and unique events. At all events, we must find a way which achieves the goal, and I have my own thoughts about that. The Jews are also extremely harmful to us through the amount of food they gorge. We have an estimated 2.5 million Jews in the Government General; if one includes those married to them and all their dependents, perhaps 3.5 million. We cannot shoot these 3.5 million Jews, we cannot poison them, but we must be able to intervene in a way which somehow achieves a successful extermination, and do so in the context of the major measures to be discussed in relation to the Reich. The Government General must be just as free of Jews as the Reich is."

So, the anticipation was there for those who were going to attend this important conference at Wannsee. At that conference, presided over by Heydrich, it was made clear that resettlement meant physical extermination. I should point out that this meeting lasted just a little bit over an hour. It was attended by just over a dozen people. Himmler wasn't present, Hitler wasn't present, Goebbels wasn't present, Goering wasn't present. These were men from positions in the party and in the state—Nazis all, of course—whose agencies would have to be involved in the direct execution of this "final solution." And Heydrich was in charge of the conference.

There would be special concentration camps created, he told them, *vernichtungslager*, death camps. In distinction from those camps in Germany, horrible enough, the sole purpose of these camps was to be the extermination of the Jews. They were to be created in Poland and others expanded, others beyond Poland: Czechoslovakia and elsewhere—prison camps, really, to handle the hundred of thousands, indeed millions, that would be transported there. Many, he said, would die in transit; others would be worked to death. The others, who had no particular value to the Reich or to the war effort, would simply be liquidated. What did that mean? It meant that mothers, small children, the old, the infirm were in principle deemed unfit for work. They would be the first to go. They would be marched directly, instantly, to their deaths at arrival at these camps. Special gas chambers would be created, special installations using Cyclon B gas, to exterminate those who were selected for transport.

In conclusion, Heydrich was talking about literally the roundup and transport of all European Jews to these death camps in the east. This was to be the "final solution." The need for secrecy was emphasized, both at Wannsee and in all subsequent operations. Why? The first reason given was that the German public simply was not prepared for this, that even some National Socialists might be shocked at the radicalism of this decision. It was necessary—certainly the Germans at home knew that something was going on. Germans living back in the Reich didn't assume that resettlement in the east for Jews meant that they were going on some sort of holiday or that they were going to the creation of new towns, new villages, new cities. But this was to be kept secret. There could be rumors; there would be rumors in Germany, but there would be no confirmation. The emphasis was on secrecy. They would not understand, Heydrich implied.

And then there was the issue that we addressed earlier, when Heydrich was concerned about the activities of the *Einsatzgruppen*: foreign propaganda. During the First World War, the Allies, the Western Allies in particular, had made great propaganda hay out of a number of incidents in Belgium, creating stories that the Germans were bayoneting babies in Belgium, that the Hun was loose in Europe. Heydrich wanted to avoid that; Hitler also was concerned about this. Heydrich wanted to avoid that, although the foreign propaganda aspect of this was not really first and foremost on his mind. Keeping it as secret as possible from the population at home was there, and then also something else that we've also alluded to, about his concerns about the activities of the *Einsatzgruppen*.

If Jews were going to be rounded up in France, in Holland, in Belgium, in Italy, in Hungary, all over German-occupied Europe, the process, Heydrich believed, would depend to a certain extent on the ignorance of the victims. They were going to be required to come to the train stations—escorted of course by *Gestapo* or SS—but it was important for those people to believe that they were off on a journey, that they were going to be resettled. They might have heard rumors about what awaited them at the end of the train line, but they certainly shouldn't have any sort of hard information. This had to be kept secret if this whole diabolical scheme was to succeed.

It was then in the spring of 1942 that the Germans launched, in this atmosphere of secrecy, the "final solution" to the Jewish question: the construction of the camps in the east. Belzec, a camp near Lublin, opened in March of 1942; Treblinka, 50 miles from Warsaw, in July of 1942; and of course Auschwitz, which already existed but which housed primarily Russian prisoners of war; indeed, the first experiments with the new gas installations would be conducted on 300 to 400 Russian prisoners who were already at Auschwitz. It was to be expanded and turned into a massive killing machine. On July 22, 1942, deportations from the Warsaw ghetto began; the destination was Treblinka.

The death camps would operate roughly with the same principles. As I said, mothers, small children, the old, the infirm were to be selected at the very beginning. The trains would arrive, many of the people coming in cattle cars, stuffed in, from various locations in Europe. On the platform, they would be separated. Those who were capable of work would be sent off in one direction; those who were deemed unfit for work into another. For those who were selected for instant death, they were told, "You've had a long journey. It's been difficult; we understand that. Be sure that you've got your luggage marked carefully, so that you'll be able to reclaim it. First you're going to need a shower. You're going to need a chance to recover." They were instructed to undress. Women and girls had their hair cut. Why? Human hair would be used for industrial purposes by the SS and their various factories, both at Auschwitz and elsewhere.

Then they were marched between files of auxiliary police, often SS people but mostly volunteers or people drafted—Poles and others— for this deadly task. They were taken down into a bunker-like room, a vast shower arrangement. They were pushed in one person at a time. The SS had calculated one person per square foot. At some point during this process, with the showerheads above them and the crush of bodies becoming greater and greater and greater, until people were jammed in shoulder to shoulder, stomach to stomach, panic would often break out among the people, either from claustrophobia or just terror at what was awaiting them. Then the great steel door at the back of the chamber would be slammed shut and barred. And then, from vents above them in the ceiling, the gas would be released into this vast chamber.

The dying took anywhere from 10 to 30 minutes for everyone to perish. Only when the last screams and cries had been heard and several more minutes had been passed were the steel doors of the chambers opened, and locals sent in—volunteers, some SS personnel—sent in, to begin the process of cleaning up bodies. Anything of value from the bodies—gold teeth, hair, anything that could be used in any way for the economic or financial uses of the regime—was claimed from those bodies.

Between 1942 and late '44, very early '45, when the camps would cease their killing, about 4 million Jews would die. Two million had already died in the activities of the *Einsatzgruppen* in Poland and Russia, bringing the total to six...six million? Seven million? No one really knows; eight million is often the high figure given, but the numbers are astronomical and beyond comprehension. Along with the Jews, Russians, Poles, gypsies would vanish into the gas chambers and then into the ovens. What one saw was the true racial essence of National Socialism. This was at the core of Nazi ideology. Those people who were deemed as enemies of the Reich, those deemed to be dangerous bacilli that would infect the healthy body of the *volk*, were now to be removed, and the beginning of this creation of a master race, which might take a thousand years, begun.

The Allies began to get information about the camps. They had already heard about the activities of the *Einsatzgruppen*, the barbaric pogroms conducted by the *Einsatzgruppen*; this they already had known about. There would certainly be reports—intelligence smuggled out of Poland about various aspects of the camps in late '42 and into 1943—but it was really 1944 before hard information became really available to the governments. Then there was a good deal of resistance to what it actually meant. For one thing, German interaction, military interaction with the Western Allies—fighting the British in northern Africa and then in '42 fighting the Americans there, and then later on, even in Western Europe after the D-Day landings in June of 1944—the German military had fought according to the accepted rules of war. There was not much evidence until late '44, when groups, German military from the east, were transferred to the West to deal with the invasion, did the Western Allies encounter real atrocities.

And so these stories coming out of the east appeared fantastic, unbelievable, Then finally, the information just was overwhelming, but then the question was, "Do what?" What to do? In August of 1944, the American air force bombed Buchenwald concentration camp in Germany; that is to say, they bombed the factories just to the east and just to the south of the concentration camp and did not hit the camp itself at all. Intelligence planes flew over Auschwitz and later would bomb factories close to Auschwitz. There was a debate within the Allied governments: what to do? Did one destroy the camps themselves and kill all the inmates? That was certainly one possibility.

It was a long way, and a very dangerous way, to fly all the way out to Poland in 1944, where the camps were. It was a dangerous military job, but it could have been done. The Allies, however, chose not to. They chose, instead, to take the position that the best way to save Jewish lives and those others caught in the concentration camps was to concentrate on defeating the Nazi military machine and destroy it as fast as possible, and that way bring the end of the regime, and therefore to save Jewish lives. There was considerable concern that, even if one bombed the camps, the Nazis would simply kill people in another way, as they had done in 1940 and 1941.

I think one always has to ask one's self, if you were Winston Churchill or Franklin Roosevelt, would you be willing to sign the order that would send planes to destroy the camps themselves, killing the prisoners there—thousands of lives, innocent lives? There was the possibility of destroying the railroad lines into the camps in the east, but one of the things that the Allied air forces had discovered over and over and over again is that you can destroy railroad lines on Monday and by Thursday the Germans would have them up and running again. This was even true of big railroad concentration points. So, very late, when most of the people who would die in concentration camps had already died, the Allies did make public statements to try to discourage the Germans, to say "The war's over, and you've lost, and there's going to be an accounting at the end of this war, and those people guilty of atrocities will be tried. You can count on it." But it was too late, much too late.

The Holocaust in that sense began, then, in 1942 with the camps and conducted, as I said, as much as possible in secrecy. Himmler, who visited a camp one time, was violently ill and never went back, was reported to have made a top-secret speech to his SS personnel in '44, in which he said, "I want to tell you about a very grave matter in all frankness. We can talk about it quite openly here, but we must never talk about it publicly. I mean the evacuation of the Jews, the extermination of the Jewish people. It is one of the things that one says lightly, 'the Jewish people are being liquidated,' party comrades exclaim. 'Naturally, it's our program—the isolation of the Jews, extermination. Okay, we'll do it.' And then they come, all the 80 million Germans, and every one of them has his decent Jew. Of course the others are all swines, but this particular one is an A-1 Jew. All those who talk like this have not seen it, have not gone through it. Most of you will know what it means to see 600 corpses piled up, or 500 or 1,000. To have gone through this and, except for a few instances of human weakness, to have remained decent, that has made us tough. That is a never-to-be-written, glorious page of our history." There one gets the most vivid description of the skewed, warped sense of morality that Himmler and his colleagues had.

1942 would also mark the real turning point in the war. The invasion of the Anglo-American forces of North Africa in 1942 and then, of course, the real turning point in the war in Europe, the long battle in Stalingrad, fought between October of 1942 and February of 1943, would seal the German fate in the east. There would be no more offenses in the east, and after that, there would be a long slog of Russian troops toward Germany. The Germans lost over half a million casualties at Stalingrad—dead, wounded or captured—and the end and the surrender of the 6th army in February '43 signaled the end of Hitler's designs in the east, and adumbrated the collapse of the Third Reich. The gradual but steady advance of the Red Army from the east and the remorseless pounding of German cities by the Anglo-American air forces would increase in 1943. The invasion of Italy by the Americans and the British in that year, and course the Normandy landings in June of 1944, mark the declining status of German military fortunes in this last phase of the war.

As Nazi military fortunes sagged, Nazi terror on the homefront intensified, and the concentration camps overflowed. It was in 1944 that a German resistance movement would finally form that would actually take action. On July 20, 1944, a conspiracy of military officers, clergymen, aristocrats, Socialists attempted a coup d'etat. Colonel Claus von Stauffenberg planted a bomb at a table where Hitler was speaking at his East Prussian headquarters. The bomb blew up, and killed other people in the room. Hitler, who was standing six feet from the bomb, survived. It ruptured his eardrum, badly hurt his arm, but he survived to go on. In the aftermath of that failed coup, Stauffenberg and others were hanged by piano wire or shot, and Germany now entered its last catastrophic phase of the war, as the SS ratcheted up the controls over the local population, where people were hanged from lanterns in the street for defeatist ideas.

By the turn of the new year, in 1945, the Russians were pressing relentlessly forward from the east, while in the west, the Anglo-American armies pushed out from the Normandy beachheads. Paris was liberated in August of '44 and then all of France. The Battle of the Bulge in December '44 and early '45 in the West was only a temporary setback for the Western Allies. It was the last gasp of the Third Reich. By the end of January, the Russians had pushed into Germany itself, as did the Western Allies. By April, Berlin stood cut off, the Russians 100 miles on the Oder from the capital city of Germany. In March, the Ruhr fell to the Americans, and the Rhine was crossed. And now, as the Allied armies moved into Germany itself, the ideological core of National Socialism revealed itself in all its grisly brutality.

In early April, the American third army liberated Buchenwald, five miles from Weimar. In April, British forces freed 55,000 inmates, miraculously still alive in Belsen. Mass graves, bodies piled in heaps, the living little more than skeletons. Ovens choked still with bodies, storage bins of gold from extracted teeth, balls of women's hair, spectacles by the thousand, dentures, clothing—including, in one camp, thousands of pairs of baby shoes—yielded up the harvest of the Third Reich.

By April 25, the Russians had reached Berlin, and on April 30, Adolf Hitler committed suicide in his bunker. In his political testament dictated shortly before he committed suicide, he stated, unregenerate to the last, "It is not true that I or anyone else in Germany wanted war in 1939. It was desired and provoked exclusively by those international statesmen who are either of Jewish ancestry or who worked for the Jewish interests. Centuries may pass, but out of the ruins of our cities and cultural monuments, hatred again will rise against that people who are ultimately responsible: international Jewry and its accomplices."

By the first week of May 1945, the Third Reich had ceased to exist. The roll call of the dead was unbelievable: 55 million people had perished in the Second World War: 1,800,000 military dead in Germany, 1,240,000 missing; 500,000 German civilians killed, largely through Allied bombing; 4 million evacuees from the east who simply vanished somewhere after the war; 390,000 British; 800,000 French; 4,500,000 Poles, civilians overwhelmingly; and Russians, 11 million military dead, 2.5 million Russian prisoners of war died in German captivity. Seven million civilians were killed by the Germans; 10 percent of the Russian population, not counting the Jews, died in the Second World War, in addition, of course, to the 6 million.

On May 2, 1945, the Third Reich ceased to exist. When the last Anglo-American bomb had been dropped on central Europe, and the last Russian shell had landed, and the German people began emerging from their hiding places to survey the smoking heaps of rubble that had once been Berlin or Dresden or Hamburg, there must have been a moment, however fleeting, when the grisly reality of all that had happened fell in upon them, and they asked themselves the question, "How had it ever come to this?" It was a question that must have haunted the ghostlike human shells that suffered the unspeakable agonies of Auschwitz or Buchenwald or Treblinka. It must have come to them in a million ways in the endless nights and days in boxcars or barracks, or prison cells, or in the gas chambers themselves, when the world had become one long, shrieking nightmare.

For the Germans, that haunting question was accompanied by an enormous burden of guilt, shame, and horror at what had been done by Germans, in the name of the German people. For them, no less than the victims of National Socialism, victims whose only crime had been to be born a Jew or a Pole or a Russian, there's another legacy, a legacy that must be ours as well. It is a political, but even more a moral, imperative that this must never happen again.

In our own feeble way, we've tried to explain events in Germany, to seek answers, or at least pose questions about the rise of National Socialism. But the story is not a unique story about Germany. Its lessons, its dangers apply to us all, touch us all, especially those of us who live in democratic societies. Be vigilant about your rights. Care about the fundamental rights and human dignity of others. When the rights of any group, no matter how small, no matter how marginal, are violated, your liberty, your freedom is put at risk. Let there never be a day when we cast about in horror and have to ask the question, "How did it ever come to this?" That, more than the details of the politics, more than the social developments, more than the theories, is the point of this course. Forewarned, let us hope, is indeed forearmed.

Timeline

1871 ....Unification of German states under Otto von Bismarck as result of the Franco-Prussian War.

1914 ....Outbreak of World War I; Germany is the leading nation of the Central Powers.

1918 ....Armistice ends fighting in World War I; Germany is defeated despite the fact that no foreign troops are on her soil.

1918 ....Left and centrist "outside" parties take over German government from the abdicated Kaiser Wilhelm and create the Weimar Republic.

1919 ....The Treaty of Versailles is signed and the League of Nations is established; Germany is not allowed to join.

1919 ....The *Nationalsozialistische Deutsche Arbeiterpartei* (National Socialist German Workers' Party, or NSDAP) develops from the German Workers' Party, founded by Gottfried Feder. Its program was nationalistic, anti-Marxist, German Socialist, and anti-Semitic.

1920 ....The NSDAP issues its "25 Points of 1920" broadening its constituency, although it is still a minuscule and localized political entity, centered in Munich.

1920 ....Adolf Hitler, a World War I German enlisted soldier, emerges from obscurity to become the leader of the NSDAP.

1923	France and Belgium invade and occupy the industrial Ruhr Valley in an effort to extract war reparation payments from Germany. The government prints money to pay workers, leading to hyperinflation and failure of the currency. Economic and political life is in turmoil.
November 8, 1923	Hitler and NSDAP attempt to seize power in Bavaria and march on Berlin; the plan fails in the so-called "Beer Hall Putsch." Hitler is tried in early 1925 and sentenced to five years in prison for treason.
1924–1928	Period of relative economic recovery; hyperinflation ends in 1923, but harsh stabilization measures create undercurrent of social and political resentment in many elements of the population, which Nazis would later exploit.
1925	Hitler publishes his manifesto, *Mein Kampf* (*My Struggle*), written while imprisoned in Landsberg, and dedicates it to 16 members of the NSDAP who were killed in the abortive Beer Hall Putsch.
1925	NSDAP re-founded; Hitler is released from prison and regains party leadership.
1926	Germany admitted to the League of Nations.
1929	The Great Depression strikes with full force, causing a drop in industrial production, an increase in unemployment, and a greater deficit. The latest coalition government in

Germany collapses and elections are set for 1930.

1930 ....Nazi electoral gains, although not enough to give them power, provide enough representation to prevent any kind of consensus in the Reichstag; rule by emergency decree becomes the norm. Heinrich Brüning is the Chancellor of Germany.

1930–1932..................................Economy worsens, and NSDAP continues to build up its strength based on disillusionment with government policies. Hitler's NSDAP begins dramatic rise in regional and local elections. In elections in spring 1932, Hitler challenges Hindenburg for president, loses, but dramatically increases his national visibility and influence.

1931 ....*Sicherheitsdienst* (SD), the security service, is created by Heinrich Himmler (leader of the *Schützstaffel*, or SS).

1932 ....Franz von Papen replaces Brüning as Chancellor. Papen has little support and calls for parliamentary elections. The Nazis run the most effective campaign in German electoral history and win 38% of the vote, making them the biggest (although not the majority) party. Negotiations begin for the chancellorship. Hermann Göering of the NSDAP assumes the post of speaker of the Reichstag.

1932	Hindenburg refuses Hitler's demands for the chancellorship; Papen dissolves the Reichstag. In November elections, Nazi vote drops (to 32%) for the first time since it began its dramatic surge in 1930. Nazis worry that their constituency is dissolving. Kurt von Schleicher is appointed chancellor in December 1932.
January 1933	After a mild Nazi rebound in regional elections in January, Schleicher requests another dissolution of the Reichstag, which Hindenburg denies. Schleicher resigns and, on January 30, Hitler is named the chancellor of Germany.
February 1933	The Reichstag building catches fire; Hitler blames the Communists and essentially moves to end all civil liberties. In the ensuing elections (which were anything but free), the NSDAP still failed to gain a majority, but were joined by Conservatives in a "Government of National Concentration."
1933	Hermann Goering creates the *Geheime Staatspolizei* (secret state police), or Gestapo, and in 1934, unites it with the SD. In essence, this move creates two terrorist police agencies, the quasi-military SS (virtually a private police force for Himmler) and the civilian Gestapo.
March 1933	The Enabling Act gives Hitler full dictatorial powers. The Weimar Republic comes to an end and the Third Reich begins.

April 1933	Legislation is enacted to eliminate Jews from the civil service. Other discriminatory steps against the German Jewish population are taken at local level between 1933 and 1935.
July 1933	The Nazis ban all political parties except the NSDAP, thus creating the foundation of a totalitarian state in Germany.
June 1934	"Blood purge" of the *Sturmabteilung* (SA); Ernst Roehm, former Chancellor Kurt von Schleicher, and other key rivals, real or imagined, are executed. Hitler passes an *ex post facto* law stating that the action was legal to defend the German state. This action removes a key competitor to the German army, which begins to rebuild.
August 1934	President Hindenburg dies; the offices of president and chancellor are united and Hitler assumes both, taking the title of *Führer*.
1935	"Nuremberg Laws" deprive German Jews of their civil rights by stripping them of citizenship, prohibiting intermarriage with Jews, and barring Jews from certain professions.
1935	Hitler creates the *Luftwaffe* (German Air Force) and introduces conscription to build a German army, both against the terms of the Treaty of Versailles.
1936	Germany re-militarizes the Rhineland, in violation of the Treaty of Versailles and other conventions.

1936 ....The Olympic Games are held in Berlin, bestowing a degree of legitimacy on Hitler's government.

1936–1939................................Hitler sends troops to Spain to assist Franco's Nationalists. This provides training for the German military, especially the *Luftwaffe.*

November 5, 1937.....................Hitler, in secret discussion with military and foreign office officials, spells out his plan for attaining *Lebensraum* (or "living room") in the east by 1943–1945.

1938 ....Austria seeks international guarantees for security but is annexed by Hitler in the *Anschluss* ("union").

1938 ....Czechoslovakia mobilizes its forces, fearing German attack on its territory over the Sudetenland; Mussolini supports Hitler's claims to the Sudetenland. The Munich Pact, brokered by Neville Chamberlain among Germany, France, England, and Italy, gives the Sudetenland to Germany.

November 10, 1938....................*Kristallnacht* ("Night of Broken Glass"), state-sponsored anti-Jewish thuggery; hundreds of Jews are killed or injured and thousands of businesses and homes, as well as synagogues, are damaged or destroyed. This action accentuated government efforts to seize Jewish assets and remove Jews from economic life in Germany.

1939–1941................................Forced expulsions and other repressive acts committed against the Jews by the Nazis. In 1939, handicapped children and mentally ill adults are killed, until public outrage stops this in August 1941. The "final solution" begins in 1941, marking the systematic state genocide of over six million people, mostly (but not entirely) Jews.

March 1939 ....Germany invades Czechoslovakia, violating the Munich Pact of the previous year, and Britain and France offer Warsaw guarantee to defend the Polish state.

August 1939 ....Hitler and Stalin sign a non-aggression pact (which contains secret provisions for dividing up Poland).

September 1939 ....Germany invades Poland, triggering World War II.

April 1940 ....Germany invades Norway and Denmark.

May 1940 ....German forces attack France, bypassing the Maginot Line.

July 1940....................................Germany plans an invasion of Britain and launches an air campaign (the Battle of Britain), involving bombing of civilian targets.

June 1941 ....Germany abrogates its non-aggression pact and launches Operation Barbarossa, the largest land invasion of history, against the Soviet Union.

December 1941 ....Soviet forces stabilize their position and stop Nazi advance near Moscow; *Blitzkrieg* phase of the war is over.

December 7, 1941 ....Japanese naval forces strike U.S. forces in Hawaii in a surprise attack. On December 11, Hitler declares war on the United States.

1942 ....Allies adopt a "Germany First" policy and plan invasions to regain territory and take the war to Germany.

1942–1945 ....Germans carry out the "final solution," aimed at Jews, gypsies, handicapped and mentally ill, homosexuals, and other "undesirables." Estimates range from six million to nine million victims.

January 1943 ....Soviet forces stop the German advance at Stalingrad and go over to the offensive on the eastern front.

June 1944 ....Allies invade France at Normandy in the largest amphibious operation in history.

December 1944 ....Battle of the Bulge in the Ardennes Forest blunts a German counteroffensive and enables Allied forces to push on for Berlin.

April 30, 1945 ....Hitler commits suicide in his bunker beneath the Reichstag as Soviet forces move into Berlin.

May 1945 ....Germany surrenders to the Allies, ending the "Thousand Year Reich" after just 12 horrifying years. Many German war leaders are subsequently tried for war crimes; several were executed and others were imprisoned for their roles in perpetrating Nazi horrors.

Biographical Notes

Brüning, Heinrich (1885–1970). Chancellor of the Weimar government for two years (1930–1932). He was appointed by President Hindenburg to cope with the severe economic problems besetting Germany during the Great Depression. He failed to gain political or popular support for his harsh fiscal policies, but served on until replaced by Fritz von Papen (q.v.) in June 1932. Unlike Papen, he left Germany after Hitler's rise to power and taught in the United States. He returned to his homeland in 1951, where he continued his academic career at the University of Cologne.

Chamberlain, Neville (1869–1940). Conservative Party Prime Minister of Great Britain from 1937 to 1940. His policy of "appeasement" was based on his hopes for preserving the peace and the poor state of British military readiness with which to confront continental dictators, such as Hitler and Mussolini. Through his role in brokering the Munich Pact, Germany was allowed to snap up Czechoslovakia, but Chamberlain realized that further territorial designs by Germany had to be forestalled. His guarantee of protection to Poland brought Great Britain into armed conflict when Germany invaded that nation on September 1, 1939, precipitating World War II. He didn't fare well as a war leader and was replaced by Winston Churchill in May 1940, dying soon thereafter.

Churchill, Winston (1874–1965). Having long warned against Hitler's aggressive ambitions in Europe, Churchill became Prime Minister of Great Britain in May 1940. He was an inspiring wartime leader, especially in the dark days of 1940, when Britain stood alone, and was tireless in his efforts to forge a great coalition against Nazi Germany. In 1941, when the Soviet Union and the United States entered the war, Churchill became the driving force in the grand alliance. His influence with Roosevelt and Stalin decreased late in the war, and he was voted out of office in the summer of 1945, before the Japanese had been defeated. He remains the very embodiment of Britain's will to survive the Nazi onslaught and, ultimately, to prevail.

Goebbels, Joseph (1897–1945). A brilliant propagandist, Goebbels emerged in 1930 as the head of the NSDAP's Propaganda Department and was responsible for planning and executing the Nazi campaigns of 1930–1932. With Hitler's appointment as chancellor,

Goebbels began Minister of Propaganda and Enlightenment and designed Nazi propaganda for the remainder of the Third Reich. Goebbels was prime organizer of the "Night of Broken Glass" in November 1938, the first coordinated nationwide act of public violence against the German Jewish community. He and his family committed suicide in Hitler's Berlin bunker in April 1945.

Goering, Hermann (1893–1946). Like Himmler, Goering was an early follower of Hitler's, taking part in the abortive Beer Hall Putsch in November 1923. Like Hitler, he was a World War I veteran, having served as a combat flyer. When Hitler came to power, Goering was given the task of building up the Gestapo (1933–1934), the *Luftwaffe* (beginning in 1935), and the Office of the Four-Year Plan (1936). He was designated *Reichsmarschall* in 1939 and was second in succession (although Himmler actually had more power). His record as head of the *Luftwaffe* was inconsistent and his influence waned as the war went on. He was captured by the American forces, tried at Nuremberg, and sentenced to be hanged, but he poisoned himself before the execution.

Heydrich, Reinhard (1904–1942). A powerful subordinate of Himmler's in the Reich Security Office, Heydrich was the architect of the "final solution of the Jewish question." In 1941, he drafted the plans for the systematic murder of the Jewish population of Europe, which he announced in a top secret gathering of select party officials in January 1942 in the Berlin suburb of Wannsee. He was killed by the Czech underground later in that year.

Himmler, Heinrich (1900–1945). An early political associate of Hitler's who took part in the Beer Hall Putsch, Himmler rose to become the second most powerful man in the Nazi hierarchy. In 1929, he became head of the *Schützstaffel*, or SS, and was instrumental in the ruthless suppression of the rival SA in the blood purge of June 30, 1934, which saw the liquidation of Ernst Roehm and other SA leaders. As head of the SS, he was responsible for carrying out Hitler's anti-Semitic policies in occupied Poland and Russia. Later in the war, he accreted additional powers. Captured by British forces after the war, he committed suicide before he could be brought to trial for war crimes.

Hindenburg, Paul von (1847–1934). A German field marshal and president from 1925 to 1934 during the Weimar Republic. His military service spanned the period from the Austro-Prussian War

(1866), the Franco-Prussian War (1870–1871), and after coming out of retirement, World War I, where he eventually became commander of all German armies. After the war, he served as president of the Weimar government, succeeding Freiderich Ebert in 1925. It was he who appointed Adolf Hitler chancellor in 1933, thus effectively ending the Weimar Republic and launching the Nazi era.

Hitler, Adolf (1889–1945). Führer of the NSDAP and Third Reich. Although not by birth a German, he came to be identified with Germany by his rise to power as head of the Nazi Party. He served in the German army in World War I, winning an Iron Cross for bravery. After the war, he became involved in politics in Bavaria, eventually taking over leadership of the small right-wing extremist National Socialist party. This group tried to take power, but its attempt was crushed in the "Beer Hall Putsch" in Munich in November 1923 and Hitler was imprisoned. While incarcerated, he wrote his manifesto, *Mein Kampf.* Upon release, he again involved himself in politics. He had learned from the putsch that the best way to gain power was constitutionally, which he succeeded in doing in a series of elections, culminating in his appointment as chancellor in January 1933. In the course of 1933–1934, Hitler laid the foundations of a totalitarian regime in Germany, transforming the Weimar Republic into the Third Reich. Under his leadership, the Nazi regime pursued a course of rabid anti-Semitism and racism, as well as an aggressive foreign policy that would lead to the outbreak of the Second World War in Europe and a fanatical and systematic campaign to destroy the Jews. He committed suicide on April 30, 1945, as Allied forces closed in on Berlin.

Papen, Franz von (1879–1969). An obscure Center Party politician, Papen was appointed by President Hindenburg to serve as German Chancellor, succeeding Heinrich Brüning (q.v.) in June 1932. During his brief tenure, he attempted to undermine the political and social foundations of the Weimar Republic, unintentionally abetting the Nazi cause. He was replaced by Kurt von Schleicher (q.v.) in November 1932 but was instrumental in bringing about Hitler's appointment as chancellor in 1933. He served as Hitler's vice-chancellor in 1933 and later as ambassador to Austria, playing a significant part in the Nazi absorption of that country.

Ribbentrop, Joachim (1893–1946). A relative latecomer to the NSDAP's hierarchy, Ribbentrop became foreign minister in 1938.

During 1938–1939, he advocated an aggressive policy, certain that Great Britain would not risk war with Germany over Austria, the Sudetenland, or even Poland. The high point of his career was the Nazi-Soviet Pact in August 1939, which paved the way for Germany's invasion of Poland. Thereafter, his influence waned. He was convicted at Nürnberg after the war and executed.

Schleicher, Kurt von (1882–1934). A military man who was prominent in the post-World War I *Reichswar*, he served as war minister to Chancellor von Papen (q.v.). He then succeeded von Papen as Chancellor and tried to forestall further Nazi political gains through dissolution of the Reichstag and assumption of emergency powers, which President Hindenburg disapproved. He resigned as chancellor in January 1933 and was replaced by Adolf Hitler. Schleicher fell victim to the blood purge of 1934, when Hitler eliminated his enemies and rivals.

Speer, Albert (1905–1981). Much admired by Hitler as a young architect, Speer designed numerous building projects for the regime, including the much- photographed stadium at Nürnberg for the NSDAP's annual rally there. During the war, he emerged as Hitler's Minister of Armaments and Munitions and is credited with having brought the war economy under control and dramatically increasing German munitions production. Sentenced to 20 years at Nürnberg after the war, he was released in 1966 and enjoyed a lucrative career as a writer and lecturer on his experiences in the Third Reich.

Stalin, Josef (1879–1953). Leader of the Soviet Union who agreed to a non-aggression pact with Hitler in August 1939. The secret terms of this pact enabled him to annex part of Polish territory in September 1939 after Hitler invaded from the west. In June 1941, Hitler invaded Russia (Operation Barbarossa). This invasion was blunted by December 1941 in the vicinity of Moscow and again at Stalingrad in late 1942 to early 1943. Russian forces went over to the offensive and eventually entered Berlin in 1945. As one of the Big Three Allied leaders, Stalin used his power and political cunning to help prepare for post-war Soviet occupation of much of Eastern Europe.

Strasser, Gregor (1892–1934). During the Weimar era, Strasser was the second-in-command of the NSDAP. A tireless campaigner, he advocated a sustained effort to win the German working class for the Nazi cause. After the November elections of 1932 brought a sudden

©2001 The Teaching Company.

decline in Nazi popularity, he withdrew from the party leadership in protest of Hitler's failure to enter a coalition government. He was among those killed by the Nazis during the "Night of Long Knives" in June 1934.

Streicher, Julius (1885–1946). Editor of a scurrilous anti-Semitic newspaper, *Der Stürmer*, and the party chief of Franconia, Streicher was the most vile of all the Nazi anti-Semites. His tireless efforts to eliminate the Jews from German life, expressed in particularly vulgar, even obscene, cartoons and editorials in *Der Stürmer*, would contribute mightily to the enactment of the Nürnberg Laws in 1935. Even loyal Nazis found him and his paper an embarrassment. He was one of Hitler's favorites.

Stresemann, Gustav (1878 –1929). A respected leader of the Weimar Republic who, both as chancellor and foreign minister, sought to reintegrate Germany into the community of nations, especially in the period 1924–1928. His untimely death in 1929 was a blow to the cause of democracy in Germany.

Bibliography

Abel, Theodore. *Why Hitler Came into Power*. Cambridge, MA: Harvard University Press, 1986. Originally published in 1936, Abel's book was based on essays written by Nazi party members who had joined the NSDAP before 1933. Abel was the first to recognize that the party's base of support went far beyond the lower middle class.

Allen, William S. *The Nazi Seizure of Power*. New York: F. Watts, 1984. Allen's excellent case study of Nordheim is the most widely taught book on the Third Reich in the United States. By analyzing the campaigns of the Nazis in a small Hannoverian town and the party's actions during 1933–1934, Allen breathes life into these tumultuous years.

Arendt, Hannah. *The Origins of Totalitarianism*. New York: Harcourt Brace Jovanovich, 1973. Arendt's classic book was among the first to develop the conception of totalitarianism. The book first appeared in the early fifties and much information has come to light since, but Arendt's brilliant work remains the most rigorous treatment of totalitarianism.

Breitman, Richard. *The Architect of Genocide: Himmler and the Final Solution*. New York: Knopf, 1991. Using hitherto unanalyzed documents, Breitman examines Himmler's role in designing the "final solution."

————. *Official Secrets: What the Nazis Planned, What the British and Americans Knew*, New York: Hill and Wang, 1998. Another important contribution to the history of the Third Reich by Breitman, this work seeks to answer the questions posed in the title.

Browning, Christopher. *Ordinary Men: Reserve Battalion 101 and the Final Solution in Poland*. New York: HarperCollins, 1992. An analytic, yet emotionally searing treatment of the "ordinary men" who served in the *Einsatzgruppen* and murdered thousands of Jews. Of the mountain of books on the Holocaust, this is one of the very best.

Bullock, Alan. *Hitler: A Study in Tyranny*. New York: Harper and Row, 1962. Although dated in some ways, Bullock's well-written and pioneering biography of Hitler remains one of the best one-volume attempts to capture Hitler and his times.

Burleigh, Michael. *The Third Reich*. New York: Hill & Wang, 2000. Burleigh has written important works on Nazi racial policy; this new book is the most recent of the synthetic histories of the Third Reich. It is also one of the best.

Childers, Thomas. *The Nazi Voter: The Social Foundations of Fascism in Germany, 1919–1933*. Chapel Hill, NC: University of North Carolina Press, 1983. One of the first books to argue that the sources of Nazi support in Germany were far broader than the lower middle class. It argues that by 1932, the NSDAP had become a "catchall party of protest."

Friedländer, Henry. *The Origins of Nazi Genocide: From Euthanasia to the Final Solution*. Chapel Hill, NC: University of North Carolina Press, 1995. Henry Friedländer has written an excellent history of the evolution of Nazi racial policy that traces it from its ideological origins to the execution of the "final solution."

Friedländer, Saul. *Nazi Germany and the Jews: The Years of Persecution, 1933–1939*. New York: Harper Collins, 1997. Friedländer's volume is the best treatment of Nazi racial policy in the years before the Second World War. A second volume, which carries this chilling story to its horrific conclusion, is expected soon.

Gellately, Robert. *The Gestapo and German Society: Enforcing Racial Policy, 1933–1945*. New York: Oxford University Press, 1990. Gellately's book examines how the Gestapo interacted with the German population, revealing that contrary to popular belief—then and now—the Gestapo was quite small and relied heavily on denunciations, often anonymous, from private citizens.

Goldhagen, Daniel. *Hitler's Willing Executioners: Ordinary Germans and the Holocaust*. New York: Alfred E. Knopf, 1997. A highly controversial treatment of National Socialist racial policy that argues that anti-Semitism was deeply engrained in German society and that the regime, far from hiding its crimes against the Jews, could count on a tradition of "eliminationist anti-Semitism" in its vicious campaign against the Jewish community.

Hitler, Adolf. *Mein Kampf*. Trans. by Ralph Manheim. Boston: Houghton Mifflin, 1971 (originally copyrighted in Germany in 1925). Virtually unreadable in its entirety, it is nonetheless a useful tool in understanding Hitler's thought and his many hatreds. Perhaps its most interesting sections deal with propaganda and organization, which anticipate modern marketing techniques.

Kaplan, Marion. *Between Dignity and Despair: Jewish Life in Nazi Germany*. New York: Oxford University Press, 1998. Kaplan's examination of everyday life in the Jewish community during the Third Reich is a powerful book and a marvelous read.

Keegan, John. *The Second World War*. London: Penguin, 1989. This volume is the most intelligent and authoritative analysis of the Second World War by the most distinguished military historian writing in English today.

Kershaw, Ian. *The Nazi Dictatorship: Problems and Perspectives of Interpretation*. 3rd ed. New York: E. Arnold (distributed by Routledge), 1993. This set of essays is devoted to the major historiographical controversies that have swirled around Hitler and the Third Reich over the years. The book is an excellent introduction to the various interpretations that have been posed and is a must read.

———. *Hitler: 1889–1936 Hubris*. New York: Norton, 1999, and *Hitler: 1936–1945 Nemesis*. New York: Norton, 2000. The two volumes of Kershaw's monumental biography of Hitler add fresh details and important new insights to our understanding of Hitler's political and personal development. It is biography at its very best.

Klemperer, Viktor. *I Will Bear Witness: The Nazi Years, 1933–1941*. New York: Random House, 1998, and *I Will Bear Witness: The Nazi Years, 1942–1945*. New York: Random House, 1999. Viktor Klemperer's secret diaries make a poignant and insightful companion to Marion Kaplan's work on Jewish life in Nazi Germany. They tell the tale of Klemperer's life in Dresden during the Third Reich and make for powerful and sometimes heartbreaking reading.

Kogon, Eugen. *The Theory and Practice of Hell*. New York: Farrar Strauss, 1950 (reprinted by Berkley, 1998). This is an older book but still one of the very best treatments of Nazi concentration camps inside Germany (Buchenwald, Dachau, Sachsenhause, and so on) by a man who spent seven years in Buchenwald.

Levi, Primo. *Survival in Auschwitz: The Nazi Assault on Humanity*. New York: Simon and Schuster, 1996 ed. Primo Levi was a survivor of Auschwitz and his book is a wrenching, yet clear-eyed account of life inside the Third Reich's most murderous death camp. It is essential reading for anyone who wants to understand how men and women coped with the cruelest of all environments.

Lukacs, John. *The Duel: Hitler vs. Churchill, 10 May–31 July 1940*. The Bodley Head, 1990 (reprinted by Phoenix Press, London). This is a very readable, probing, and provocative account of the showdown between Germany and Britain during the crucial months of 1940.

————. *Five Days in London, May 1940*. New Haven, CT: Yale University Press, 1999. Following up on *The Duel*, Lukacs dissects the critical early days of Churchill's prime ministership, emphasizing the precarious position Churchill was in, not only with regard to the German menace but to opposition in Britain as well.

Mommsen, Hans. *The Weimar Republic*. Chapel Hill, NC: University of North Carolina Press, 1995. Over his long career, Hans Mommsen has been perhaps the best historian of Weimar and the Third Reich, and this treatment of the Weimar Republic may be his crowning achievement.

Overy, Richard J. *Russia's War*. London: Penguin, 1997. The basis of a BBC series on the war on the eastern front, Overy's book is a very readable, incisive, and thoughtful analysis of a side of the war that is frequently underappreciated in the West.

————. *Why the Allies Won*. New York: Norton, 1995. Written by one of the best historians of the Second World War, this is an interrelated series of essays about the war economy, the quality of leadership, military strategy, and the domestic societies of the major combatants in the Second World War.

Peukert, Detlev. *Inside the Third Reich: Conformity and Opposition*. New Haven, CT: Yale University Press, 1987. An untimely death cut short the career of Detlev Peukert, one of the most innovative historians of 20th-century Germany. This book offers a provocative analysis of resistance, opposition, and dissent in the Third Reich, probing areas of social life and behavior hitherto unexamined.

Speer, Albert. *Inside the Third Reich*. London: Sphere Books, 1971. Speer, Hitler's architect and later leader of the German war economy, offers an inside account of life at the highest levels of the Third Reich. It is especially valuable for its portrayal of the "organized chaos" that characterized so much of Nazi administrative organization.

Taylor, A. J. P. *The Origins of the Second World War*. London: Penguin, 1961. This highly controversial account of Hitler's foreign policy and the international responses to it is brilliant in its explanation of French and English policy and maddeningly myopic in dealing with Hitler's. After all these years, it remains an important book and a fascinating read.

Trevor-Roper, Hugh. *The Last Days of Hitler.* New York: Macmillan, 1947. (reprinted by Pan Books, 1973).

Turner, Henry A., Jr. *Big Business and the Rise of Hitler.* New York: Oxford University Press, 1985. Turner undermines the once popular notion that Hitler was a stooge for big business in the critical years before 1933. Turner demonstrates convincingly that the NSDAP did not benefit significantly from corporate contributions and that the business elites were ambivalent at best about Hitler's economic and social positions.

——. *Hitler's Thirty Days to Power: January 1933.* Reading, MA: Addison Wesley, 1996. A penetrating examination of Hitler's appointment as chancellor in January 1933, Turner's book emphasizes the role of chance and personality in that momentous event.

Notes

Notes